On Violence in History

On Violence in History

Edited by

Philip Dwyer

Mark S. Micale

berghahn

NEW YORK · OXFORD

www.berghahnbooks.com

Published in 2020 by
Berghahn Books
www.berghahnbooks.com

Originally published as a special issue of
Historical Reflections/Réflexions Historiques, volume 44, number 1.

Library of Congress Cataloging in Publication Data

Names: Dwyer, Philip G., editor. | Micale, Mark Stephen, editor.
Title: On violence in history / edited by Philip Dwyer, Mark S. Micale.
Description: First Edition. | New York : Berghahn Books, 2020. | Includes
    bibliographical references and index.
Identifiers: LCCN 2019042146 (print) | LCCN 2019042147 (ebook) | ISBN
    9781789204643 (hardback) | ISBN 9781789204650 (paperback) | ISBN
    9781789204667 (ebook)
Subjects: LCSH: Violence--History.
Classification: LCC HM1116 .O6 2020 (print) | LCC HM1116 (ebook) | DDC
    303.609--dc23
LC record available at https://lccn.loc.gov/2019042146
LC ebook record available at https://lccn.loc.gov/2019042147

British Library Cataloguing in Publication Data

A catalogue record for this book is available from the British Library

ISBN 978-1-78920-464-3 hardback
ISBN 978-1-78920-465-0 paperback
ISBN 978-1-78920-466-7 ebook

Contents

:::

Illustrations

Preface

Philip Dwyer and Mark S. Micale

S hortly before the appearance of our special issue of *Historical Reflections/
Réflexions Historiques* at the beginning of 2018, Steven Pinker published
another book, *Enlightenment Now: The Case for Reason, Science, Humanism, and
Progress*, which is essentially a response to those who criticized *The Better
Angels of Our Nature*. Bill Gates immediately declared the new volume "my
new favorite book of all time." In it, Pinker presents himself as a champion
of the values of the Enlightenment because no one else was "willing to defend them," as well as a defender of progress. Intellectuals, Pinker writes
in *Enlightenment Now*, hate "the *idea* of progress".[1] By that he means, "the
Enlightenment belief that by understanding the world we can improve the
human condition."

Enlightenment Now has been heavily critiqued. If in *The Better Angels* we
are living in the most peaceful era in human history, life is simply getting
better in *Enlightenment Now*. In it, Pinker argues that "we" are much better
off due to "newborns who will live more than eight decades, markets over-
flowing with food, clean water that appears with a flick of a finger and waste
that disappears with another, pills that erase a painful infection, sons who
are not sent off to war, daughters who can walk the streets in safety, critics of
the powerful who are not jailed or shot, the world's knowledge and culture
available in a shirt pocket."[2]

Much of that is debatable. Oxfam tells us that 1,000 children per day
will die of contaminated water; there are certainly a few countries where
sons are still sent off to war, where journalists are imprisoned or killed for
speaking truth to power, and many more where it is not safe for women to
walk the streets at night. According to a recent UNHCR report, there were
68.5 million forcibly displaced people in the world, including 25.4 million
refugees, approaching levels not seen since World War II. Pinker, in other

words, has gone on the offensive, apparently eschewing the many well-informed and often-valid criticisms made of *The Better Angels of Our Nature*, and ignoring scholars who have pointed to any number of historical inaccuracies dotted throughout the book. In an interview conducted by a journalist for the British newspaper, *The Guardian*, on the occasion of the appearance of *Enlightenment Now*, Pinker doubled down, hitting back at his critics:

> One of the surprises in presenting data on violence," he says, "was the lengths to which people would go to deny it. When I presented graphs showing that rates of homicide had fallen by a factor of 50, that rates of death in war had fallen by a factor of more than 20, and rape and domestic violence and child abuse had all fallen, rather than rejoice, many audiences seemed to get increasingly upset. They racked their brains for ways in which things could not possibly be as good as the data suggested, including the entire category of questions that I regularly get: Isn't X a form of violence? Isn't advertising a form of violence? Isn't plastic surgery a form of violence? Isn't obesity a form of violence?[3]

Pinker's response is disingenuous and fails to engage the more serious criticisms of *The Better Angels*, many of which can be found in our book. As we learn in the following chapters, it is easy enough to critique how Pinker does history as well as the types of data he uses, and the uses to which he puts that data.

There are, furthermore, two larger implications to this kind of overarching history of which Pinker is probably not even aware. The first has to do with "authority," or "voices of authority" if you like. This is more than just a simple difference of opinion between squabbling academics. As the Princeton historian, David Bell, pointed out in a recent article on truth and democracy, "truth, and the authority to determine it, has always been deeply contested, and that philosophers from ancient Greece onward have wrestled in profound and troubling ways with how to distinguish objective reality from human perception."[4] A question to the student, then, is how, in the face of competing sets of data and conflicting interpretations, does one determine who is "right?" The decisive point of difference may be in how one side wields "historical facts" in support of its case, while the other presents more nuanced arguments that purport to understand the past in more subtle ways.

The second has to do with the idea of "progress" in history, and what historians do with overarching explanations of history such as Pinker's. This is not the place to marshal detailed evidence, but it is worth pointing out that no Enlightenment thinker would have maintained that progress was universal and absolute. Jean-Jacques Rousseau, for example, was aware that progress and regress can coexist. That may or may not be the case, but as the human rights historian, Samuel Moyn, pointed out in a critique of Pinker's *Enlightenment Now*, citing Immanuel Kant, "the problem of progress cannot be solved directly from experience… Even if it were found that the human race as a whole had been moving forward and progressing for an indefinitely long time, no one could guarantee that its era of decline was not beginning at that very moment."[5]

We would like to thank Marion Berghahn and Amanda Horn at Berghahn Books for giving us the opportunity to reprint the special issue of *Historical Reflections/Réflexions Historiques* and thereby introducing the material in it to college audiences. We heartily thank all the journal contributors who agreed to have their work reprinted. We hope that these chapters will inspire students to think more critically about the uses to which history can be put by people who are not trained in that discipline. Finally, it is with great sadness that we learned that one of our contributors, Matthew Trundle, Professor in Classics at the University of Auckland, passed away of leukemia in July 2019.

Philip Dwyer is Professor of History and founding Director of the Centre for the Study of Violence at the University of Newcastle, Australia. He has written on the Revolutionary and Napoleonic Wars, memoirs, violence, and colonialism, and is the general editor (with Joy Damousi) of the four-volume Cambridge World History of Violence, *forthcoming from Cambridge University Press.*

Mark S. Micale is Emeritus Professor of History at the University of Illinois in Urbana-Champaign. The author or editor of seven books, his work focuses on European intellectual and medical history and the history of masculinities.

Notes

1. Steven Pinker, *Enlightenment Now: The Case for Reason, Science, Humanism, and Progress* (New York: Viking, 2018), 39.
2. Pinker, *Enlightenment Now*, 4.
3. Andrew Anthony, "Steven Pinker: 'The way to deal with pollution is not to rail against consumption,'" *The Guardian*, 11 February 2018, https://www.theguardian.com/science/2018/feb/11/steven-pinker-enlightenment-now-interview-inequality-consumption-environment.
4. David Avrom Bell, "An Equal Say. Where does truth fit into democracy?", *The Nation*, 24 January 2019, https://www.thenation.com/article/david-bell-democracy-and-truth/.
5. Samuel Moyn, "Hype for the Best: Why does Steven Pinker insist that human life is on the up?", 19 March 2018, *The New Republic*, https://newrepublic.com/article/147391/hype-best.

Introduction

History, Violence, and Steven Pinker

Mark S. Micale and Philip Dwyer

In the closing months of 2011, Harvard psychologist Steven Pinker published *The Better Angels of Our Nature: The Decline of Violence in History and
Its Causes*.[1] Weighing in at over eight hundred closely printed pages, Pinker's book advances a bold, revisionist thesis: despite the relentless deluge of
violent, sensationalist stories in the pervasive electronic media of our day,
Pinker proposes, violence in the human world, in nearly every form, has in
fact declined dramatically. Over the past several thousand years, and particularly since the eighteenth century, homicides, criminal assaults, war casualties, domestic violence, child abuse, animal abuse, capital punishment,
lynching, and rape have all been steadily diminishing in frequency.

This might at first seem illogical given that an estimated 160–180 million
people were killed as a direct result of war and genocide—consider World
Wars I and II, the Holocaust, Stalin's Russia, Mao's China, and Pol Pot's
Cambodia—but Pinker argues that killing as a per capita estimate was much
higher in previous centuries. Indeed, it appears to have been higher the further one goes back in time, so that nonstate societies in earlier centuries had
death rates of anywhere between 0 and 60 percent, with an average of 15
percent, while the total number of overall deaths in the twentieth century
represents an overall death rate of only 3 percent. To buttress this original
argument, the author assembled countless statistical "data sets" and over a
hundred charts and graphs.

With a thesis so novel and counterintuitive, presented in a tone of such
self-assurance, Pinker's book attracted a great deal of attention upon its appearance several years ago. In the United States and United Kingdom, the initial coverage included lengthy discussions in venues such as the *New Yorker,*
the *New York Times,* the *Guardian,* the *American Scholar,* the *Los Angeles Review
of Books,* the *Wall Street Journal,* the *Spectator, Slate,* the *Huffington Post, Scientific
American, Foreign Policy,* and the *Daily Telegraph.* A number of publications

ran follow-up articles. The current Wikipedia entry for Pinker's tome, which canvasses both praise for and criticism of the book, quotes from 30 reviews.[2] In these early assessments, psychologists, sociologists, anthropologists, theologians, scientists, foreign policy experts, philosophers, and popular science writers, as well as public intellectuals, all had their say. Curiously, very few academic historians were included in this first wave of critical reviewers.[3]

The absence of historians from the early commentary on Pinker's book is unfortunate. In his home disciplines of cognitive psychology and psycholinguistics, Pinker is very well-known. In numerous earlier works in these fields, he demonstrated a talent for intellectually ambitious projects, grand (if not extravagant) interpretations, and wide-ranging syntheses combined with a skill for popular scientific exposition. Unlike his earlier volumes, however, *The Better Angels of Our Nature*, in its core arguments and its key source materials, is specifically historical.

Pinker's postulation of a *longue durée* decline in human violence cites an array of horrible past practices—ranging from torture, gladiatorial displays of fighting to the death, and burning religious heretics, to breaking on the rack, tarring and feathering, and the corporal punishment of children—that have either been replaced by greater restraint or abolished altogether in modern times. Fueling this steady retreat from violent practices in the past few centuries, Pinker asserts, has been the increasing importance of empathy, self-control, social cooperation, and rational thinking in governing human affairs, rather than our species' darker and more primitive capacities for aggression, including murder.

In this process of progressive self-pacification, Pinker places special emphasis on the Enlightenment, broadly conceived, which initiated "the humanitarian revolution." The growing adoption of rationality in government, the rise of concepts of political and civil rights, the emergence of the idea of religious toleration, the development of a more cosmopolitan outlook on foreign cultures, and the consolidation of the modern nation-state with its stabilizing monopoly on the legal, legitimate use of force are among the most important civilizing, humanitarian sources of change that Pinker posits. These transformations, he continues, were reinforced by at least two other, roughly coterminous, forces: in the economic realm, an increasingly global development of the exchange of trade goods, which required cooperation rather than conflict with foreigners, and, in the world of gender, "feminization," or a growing respect for and adoption of "the interests and values of women" in contrast to the more martial, masculinist outlooks that predominated during prehistoric, ancient, and medieval eras. As every reader of this volume will readily recognize, these ideas are historical in nature, and rich and voluminous bodies of scholarship exist on all of them.

A second context for this volume transcends any one field of inquiry. In the early twenty-first century, "the history of violence" is rapidly emerging as a productive new research site at the interface of history, psychology, and anthropology, among other disciplines. Historical scholarship on violence now flourishes, including both general longitudinal surveys and specialized studies of single categories of violence and of violent activity in particular past times and places.[4] A multivolume history of violence from prehistoric times to the present is underway by Cambridge University Press.[5] More and more interdisciplinary conferences with violence as a central theme are being organized internationally. Not least significant is a burgeoning interest in the subject among university students, who often serve as excellent barometers of emerging areas of contemporary interest. Master's theses and doctoral dissertations dealing with the history of violence are proliferating, and college courses as well as graduate seminars on the subject are beginning to appear in history curricula. And in 2011, the same year Pinker's book appeared, the University of Newcastle in Australia established the first Centre for the History of Violence. Can a journal, digital bibliography, and world congress be far behind?

It is always exciting to observe the formation of a new field of historical knowledge, especially one as resonant politically and morally as this one is. As a subdiscipline first takes shape, the appropriate subject matter of the field, its basic analytical frameworks, the best methodologies to employ, and the key questions to investigate are all open for discussion. Which brings us back to Pinker. A quick check of book prefaces, article footnotes, promotional materials, conference programs, project proposals, and course syllabuses indicates that Pinker's tome is being cited extensively as a major interpretative point of departure for this new historical initiative. In fact, Pinker's *Better Angels of Our Nature* appears second only to Norbert Elias's *The Civilizing Process* in the frequency of its citation.[6] Given the sweeping breadth of its coverage, its outspoken revisionism, and the author's knack for "big ideas," this is perhaps inevitable. Furthermore, Pinker's book, it should be noted, often serves in these sources as a reading to consider, confront, and contest. Nevertheless, if Pinker's book is elevated into a founding statement in the historiography of human violence—if, that is, it constitutes a "thesis," akin in their respective historiographies to, say, the "Weber Thesis," the "Turner Frontier Thesis," the "Pirenne Thesis," the "Hobson/Lenin Thesis," or "the Boswell Thesis"—then surely the interpretation requires close and systematic evaluation by the very group of trained experts tasked by society with studying history responsibly, professionally, and institutionally.

Finally, we believe that such an intervention might be urgent, which brings us to the third motivation for this volume. Pinker's work has had such an impact on the popular imagination that historians of violence can no longer avoid it. This popular acceptance of his work came to the fore quite recently when, on 16 May 2017, a remarkable posting on the social media site Twitter appeared. The tweet came from Bill Gates, the famous Microsoft founder and one of the richest people on the planet. Gates directed his message to college students, who were then completing their studies in great numbers across North America and Europe. In his tweet, Gates recommended that all graduating students read Pinker's *Better Angels of Our Nature*.

"[Pinker] shows how the world is getting better," Gates proclaimed. "Sounds crazy but it's true. This is the most peaceful time in human history." "That matters," Gates added, "because if you think the world is getting better, you want to spread the progress to more people and places."[7] Gates went on to link the idea of a momentous long-term decline in violence with both personal happiness and an optimistic view of social modernity. In a later, even more euphoric, pronouncement Gates declared that "if I could give each of you a graduation gift, it would be this—the most inspiring book I've ever read."[8]

News of Gates's ecstatic online endorsement quickly "went viral." Many leading Anglophone newspapers reported the story, often including excerpts from Gates's comments and printing article headlines that "things are actually getting better in the world today." Indeed, we learned of Gates's tweet from a full-page article in the *Sydney Morning Herald*. The combined effect of this publicity was to catapult Pinker's book to the very top of the bestseller list on Amazon.com during the summer months of 2017.

If *Better Angels of Our Nature* helps to motivate the public generosity of a billionaire philanthropist, then that is an unexpected beneficial effect. What surely emerges from these events, however, is that Pinker's book has become a general cultural phenomenon. Its ideas are entering mainstream public discourse and are beginning to inform the activities and outlook of some of the most prominent and influential people today. For better or worse, the Pinker Thesis is spreading globally.

That is why we strongly believe—and the editorial board of *Historical Reflections* agrees—that the time is ripe for the community of academic historians to formally engage with Pinker's ideas. We have assembled a set of critical essays, written by a group of accomplished senior historians, that evaluate *The Better Angels of Our Nature* by the standards of professional historical scholarship. We have chosen our contributing authors not only because of their distinguished careers but because of the diversity of historical specialties they represent: this will allow an examination of Pinker's book, and its component parts, from as many empirical and analytical vantage points as possible. Thus, we include articles that study violence in prehistory, ancient Mediterranean societies, medieval Europe, early modern Russia, the European Enlightenment, interwar Africa and the Middle East, and European fascism. Supplementing these geochronological perspectives are thematic articles that take up sexual violence, violence and the history of science and technology, and violence and neurohistory. We are keenly aware that many additional histories (above all, of China) could profitably be included were space limitations not a concern.

Not all of the scholars included in this volume agree on everything, but the overall verdict is that Pinker's thesis, for all the stimulus it may have given to discussions around violence, is seriously, if not fatally, flawed. The problems that come up time and again are: the failure to genuinely engage with historical methodologies; the unquestioning use of dubious sources; the tendency to exaggerate the violence of the past in order to contrast it with the supposed peacefulness of the modern era; the creation of a number of straw men, which Pinker then goes on to debunk; and its extraordinarily Western-centric, not to say Whiggish, view of the world. Complex historical questions, as the essays in this volume clearly demonstrate, cannot be answered with any degree of certainty, and certainly not in a simplistic way. Our goal here is not to offer a final, definitive verdict on Pinker's work; it is, rather, to initiate an ongoing process of assessment that in the future will incorporate as much of the history profession as possible.

Mark S. Micale is Emeritus Professor of History at the University of Illinois in Urbana-Champaign. The author or editor of seven books, his work focuses on European intellectual and medical history and the history of masculinities.

Philip Dwyer is Professor of History and founding Director of the Centre for the Study of Violence at the University of Newcastle, Australia. He has written on the Revolutionary and Napoleonic Wars, memoirs, violence, and colonialism, and is the general editor (with Joy Damousi) of the four-volume Cambridge World History of Violence, *forthcoming from Cambridge University Press.*

Notes

1. Steven Pinker, *The Better Angels of Our Nature: The Decline of Violence in History and Its Causes* (London: Allen Lane, 2011).
2. Wikipedia.com, *"The Better Angels of Our Nature,"* https://en.wikipedia.org/wiki/The_Better_Angels_of_Our_Nature (accessed 22 January 2018).
3. For two exceptions, see Mark S. Micale, "Improvements," *Times Literary Supplement* (9 March 2012); and Michael Shermer, "Getting Better All the Time," *American Scholar* (Autumn, 2011), https://theamericanscholar.org/getting-better-all-the-time/#.WnKbl9QrJiw (accessed 22 January 2018).
4. For an early attempt to organize some of this scholarship historiographically, see Gregory Hanlon, "Review-Article: The Decline of Violence in the West: From Cultural to Post-Cultural History," *English Historical Review* 128, no. 531 (April 2013): 367–400, http://www.academia.edu/5038629/The_Decline_of_Violence_in_the_West_from_cultural_to_post-cultural_history_review_article.
5. Philip Dwyer and Joy Damousi, eds., *The Cambridge World History of Violence*, 4 vols. (Cambridge: Cambridge University Press, forthcoming).
6. See Norbert Elias, *The Civilizing Process: Sociogenetic and Psychogenetic Investigations*, rev. ed., trans. Edmund Jephcott (Oxford: Blackwell Publishers, 2000).
7. See Bill Gates, *gatesnotes*, "Better Angels of Our Nature in Graphs & Numbers," https://www.gatesnotes.com/About-Bill-Gates/Better-Angels-of-Our-Nature-in-Graphs-and-Numbers, and "My New Favorite Book of All Time," https://www.gatesnotes.com/Books/Enlightenment-Now (accessed 30 March 2018).
8. Billionaires seem drawn to the book. See also Rhiannon Williams, "Mark Zuckerberg's Year of Books: The Full List," *Daily Telegraph,* 1 February 2015, http://www.telegraph.co.uk/technology/mark-zuckerger/11379640/Mark-Zuckerbergs-Year-of-Books-the-full-list.html (accessed 16 January 2018).

Chapter 1

The Past as a Foreign Country
Bioarchaeological Perspectives on Pinker's "Prehistoric Anarchy"

Linda Fibiger

Steven Pinker's *The Better Angels of Our Nature* is not the first publication to have put bioarchaeological evidence for high levels of violence in prehistory into the spotlight.[1] Like Pinker, Lawrence Keeley's *War Before Civilization* gave prominence to both skeletal and ethnographic studies when re-creating the prehistoric narrative on violence, rejecting the image of a pacified past.[2] Pinker has, in fact, simply reused many of the studies featured in Keeley's work. This has come under considerable criticism on the basis of its statistical inferences, which use percentage deaths in war of up to 60 percent in some archaeological as well as ethnographic studies, and is more eloquently and knowledgably discussed by Pasquale Cirillo and Nassim Taleb and by Dean Falk and Charles Hildebolt.[3] Most recently, Rahul Oka and colleagues have demonstrated that Keeley's and Pinker's approach of simply considering the number of those engaged in violent conflict and the proportion of those killed by violent acts may not be a sufficiently robust indicator for comparisons across time. Instead, they postulate that units with larger population sizes—such as those identified as "states"—produce more casualties "per combatant than in ethnographically observed small-scale societies or in historical states." In short, this means that modern states are not any less violent than their archaeological predecessors.[4] While numbers are at the heart of much of the criticism leveled at Pinker, it is terminology that will be considered first here, followed by a critical exploration of bioarchaeological data generation, analysis, and interpretation, which provide the foundation on which much of Pinker's argument for prehistoric violence rests.

Talking about the Violent Past

Both archaeology and bioarchaeology (that is, the scientific analysis of human skeletal remains) are, as disciplines, reliant on clear, unequivocal terminology when trying to identify, classify, analyze, and interpret what is in many cases a fragmented, incomplete record to re-create past human activity. This terminology may not be universal and can include, for example, particular regional chronologies and systems of periodization, underpinned by more widely accepted conventions, ethical and professional frameworks, and operational procedures (for example, the Vermillion Accord on Human Remains).[5] This is, of course, common to many disciplines, and a failure to fully understand, apply, or cross-reference important key terms that emerge from other disciplines will ultimately obscure, confuse, or weaken a potential argument, as will the assumption of universality of meaning.

Defining Prehistory

The first term that needs to be considered critically is that of prehistory itself, which throughout Pinker's book is presented as a unifying expression mainly used to refer to nonstate societies and the "anarchy of the hunting, gathering and horticultural societies in which our species spent most of its evolutionary history to the first agricultural civilizations with cities and governments, beginning around five thousand years ago."[6] In archaeological terms, prehistory encompasses a vast period of tens of thousands of years. Its traditional periodization highlights apparent changes in aspects of materials culture (Stone Age, Bronze Age, Iron Age), and is also punctuated by shifts in subsistence (such as the introduction of agriculture), settlement patterns (permanent rather than seasonal settlements), and societal organization and administration (such as urbanization).[7] The overall characterization of prehistory immediately becomes much less defined and consistent when homing in on different regions at different times within Pinker's main chronological focus of hunter-gatherer/horticultural societies and beyond. The transition to agriculture, for example, certainly did not equal the universal emergence of cities and governments Pinker is implying.

The Danish cemetery site of Vedbæk, featured in Pinker's table documenting deaths in warfare in nonstate and state societies, is a good case in point and highlights some of the complexities behind each of the 22 sites listed by Pinker as representative of warfare deaths at prehistoric archaeological sites that, overall, make up a less than coherent sample.[8] At Vedbæk, two of the 21 burials (a small assemblage, which is not apparent when presented as percentage figures only) showed potential signs of violence. The cemetery dates to the fifth millennium BCE and is attributed to the Mesolithic (that is, hunter-gatherer dominated) Ertebølle horizon (named after its type site in Jutland), representing complex hunter-gatherer-fisher groups whose settlement sites (some of which were probably occupied year-round) and cemeteries indicate social complexity and a relatively high degree of economic stability—something conventionally associated with the Neolithic period and an agricultural subsistence economy.[9]

A single site from Denmark cannot be considered representative of Pinker's assumed nonstate prehistoric horizon in a northern European context, and it is certainly highly problematic to compare or even group it with the geographically and temporally removed sites from India, Africa, and North America that join Vedbæk in Pinker's table, selected purely, one would guess, for their already collated and published English-language availability. Even much closer to Vedbæk, across the North Sea in Britain, a completely different picture for the Mesolithic emerges. No Mesolithic cemeteries have been excavated here to date, human remains are usually found disarticulated and in a variety of mostly nonfunerary contexts, and the complete skeletal record for the whole period consists of fewer skeletal remains than the single site of Vedbæk. Skeletal remains provide the most direct evidence for violence in prehistory, especially in times and places where specialized weapons may not exist or fortified architecture is absent.[10] Of course, we can analyze them only where we find them, but it would be difficult to make a broad statement about cross-regional or continental trends of violent interaction in prehistory from the remains of 21 individuals found in a small cemetery.

Defining War

While the subtitle of Pinker's book refers to the history of violence, it is the term warfare that features large in his narrative and is applied universally to a variety of contexts and data sets, ranging from violence-related skeletal trauma data in prehistoric grave sites to death statistics from world wars. This raises the important question of the definition of the term and concept of war, what actually constitutes true evidence for its presence, and how this may vary depending on the context and period. This is an underdeveloped but important aspect in Pinker's argument.

Available definitions of war arise from anthropological, archaeological, historical, and military studies and place different emphases on social, tactical, and physical aspects, varying degrees of specificity and complexity, and different scales of conflict. Physical force and domination are recurring features in existing characterizations of war, as are its link to groups or defined units.[11] Additional identifying features frequently examined are lethality, territoriality, and duration.[12] At other times, war is defined exclusively as a state activity.[13] All of these attributes are valid and important considerations, but they are varied and not universally present in Pinker's data sample.

The scale of feuding and raiding, common expressions of conflict in pre-industrialized, preliterate, small-scale societies like those of the earlier prehistoric periods to which Pinker is referring, may well be characterized by "organized fighting" involving planning, direction, and an expected set of lasting results.[14] It may also see the application of the "use of organized force between independent groups" and therefore be defined as warfare according to some of the current anthropological definitions of war.[15] This does not mean it is always possible to distinguish its presence and results, at least archaeologically, from one-off violent events and other forms of interpersonal violence such as one-to-one fights, punishment, torture, and domestic violence. The scale and intensity of a conflict may not necessarily be accurately reflected in the archaeological record, and warfare as a scaled, organized, long-term group conflict will need critical levels of human casualties or material destruction to be visible archaeologically and/or osteologically.[16]

In the face of such different ideas about underlying concepts as well as the actual practice of war, the main function of applying the term universally across time and space appears to be its superficial simplicity, its familiarity, and its popular accessibility in a work that is situated across the popular/academic divide. Warfare also suggests a sense of scale that—when considering the discussions on Vedbæk and on the statistical validity of some of the data in Pinker's work—may be misleading. It does also, even unintentionally, dramatize, perhaps even sensationalize the topic in a way that the term violence may not to the same degree.[17]

Tribes and Tribal People

The term tribe or tribal people, as used by Pinker, is not without problems. Past criticisms have resulted from its potential colonial associations, involving assumed uniformity and linear concepts of societal development (that is, from the more "primitive" to the more "advanced/civilized").[18] The key issue arises from the quasi-evolutionary classification it may suggest in a study that contrasts the concept of tribal with apparently more developed/advanced, and therefore more peaceful, state societies. This situation is further complicated by grouping recent ethnographic data with prehistoric archaeological data, which assumes or at the very least suggests uniformity or comparability between the two, blurring the lines between a projected or theorized past (the recent ethnographic record as a good approximation of the distant past), and the actual contemporaneous record of that past (the physical and bioarchaeological evidence).

If we use the term tribe simply as a descriptive term, what does it mean? It could, for example, suggest the presence of small- or medium-sized, local, prestate groups, connected by language, culture, and subsistence practices.[19] These groups might have been interacting, and lineages or families are likely to have provided their organizational basis. This has been confirmed for later agricultural groups through DNA analysis, such as at Eulau in Germany.[20] Nor can potential for some degree of social ranking, prestige, or leadership be disregarded.[21] Again, we cannot really rely on this concept to be accurate for all the groups, past and present, summarized under nonstate societies in Pinker's work. The term's value as a descriptive shorthand, even if properly defined, may be outweighed by the potential historically derived connotations of inferior societal development, and the use of the term small-scale societies may be more appropriate in many cases.

Body Counts and Boneyards

Every scholar, every scientist, every researcher publishing their work is under public scrutiny. Even highly technical, specialized, or apparently inaccessible research results can find their way into the public sphere, and many, like *The Better Angels of Our Nature,* are created for this very purpose: as semipopular works accessible to specialists and nonspecialists alike. In this case, the book's scope beyond the author's own discipline means that the choice of terminology and language used is pivotal, not just while trying to engage diverse audiences when presenting within the author's own specialism, but also while stepping outside it. While a certain degree of compromise and loss of detail may be unavoidable in "bigger picture" studies, this should not compromise sensitivity to wider issues within and outside the discipline.

Data resulting from the excavation, analysis, and continued curation of human skeletal remains is a particularly complex and highly sensitive issue with laws, guidelines, opinions, and degrees of public approval, varying considerably regionally, nationally, and globally.[22] Pinker's assertion that "several scholars have been scouring the anthropological and historical literature for every good body count from non-state societies that they could find" is a flippant description of the research process that would not be as readily applied if he were talking of more recent victims of conflict.[23] Do historians of the twentieth century scour manuscripts and archival records for good body counts of the world war dead, or do they carry out considered archival work that respects the sensitivity of the subject? There are also the statistics that are "harder to compute from boneyards."[24] Here Pinker is referring to the burial grounds, cemeteries, and potential massacre sites that make up his archaeological sample, including a large number of Native American skeletal remains. One can hardly imagine this term being applied to Arlington National Cemetery or the war cemeteries of Flanders Fields, and its use by Pinker does suggest a lack of cultural sensitivity to deaths in the deep past, including deaths that, in this case, still matter to Native descendant groups today.

The Bioarchaeological Record

Questions of methodology and ethically sound terminology discussed so far are also at the core of human skeletal analysis. The following section is going to highlight a number of caveats and limitations affecting the use of skeletal data that have an immediate bearing on the validity and suitability of Pinker's collated data set. Some of these aspects, including high selectivity and lack of representativeness in the sample, have been touched upon in R. Brian Ferguson's recent critiques of Pinker but deserve more detailed consideration.[25]

The Missing Neolithic

Bioarchaeologists of prehistory have long known about the potential for violence in the period, long before Keeley's coverage of the subject, not least through Joachim Wahl and H. G. König's 1987 publication of the Neolithic mass grave from Talheim, Germany. The skeletal remains from the site, dating to the later phase of the earliest Neolithic in the region (c. 5000 BCE) document the violent killing of 34 individuals, including men, women, and children who were consequently buried in a pit without apparent care or consideration.[26] Overall, the current skeletal data set for the Neolithic in western and northern Europe in particular, but also for other regions in Europe, does in fact present a more comprehensive, better understood, and therefore more useful data set than the Mesolithic assemblages Pinker has focused on. Chronologically, the Neolithic fills the period between Pinker's apparent hunter-gatherer "anarchy" and what he terms the "first agricultural civilizations with cities and governments." Following Pinker's argument, this earliest phase of permanently settled agriculturalists should mark the beginnings of the decline of violent conflict. However, from bioarchaeological studies we know that in the few regions where both good Mesolithic and Neolithic skeletal remains are available, violence-related skeletal trauma frequencies do not appear to vary much at all and do not represent the peak Pinker is implying.[27] The omission of the Neolithic from Pinker's skeletal data set, even though this period marks one of the most profound subsistence and cultural changes in human history, is puzzling and unsettling, especially in view of ready data availability. It may be explained through ignorance of this data source, which seems unlikely. The omission may have more to do with the problem of how to represent the varied and extensive Neolithic data set, which will be discussed in more detail below.

Differential Diagnosis of Violence-Related Trauma and Collated Data Sets

Bioarchaeologists diagnose pathologies, including skeletal evidence for trauma, by looking at patterns of changes to the skeleton, discussing potential causes for the changes observed, and making a decision on the most likely cause for the pattern observed with consideration of the wider context of the remains (such as the chronological and biological age and the archaeological context). In suspected cases where the implement of violence is still present, as in the case of embedded projectiles, this may be an obvious process. In all other cases the likelihood of an observed injury to be diagnosed as intentional rather than accidental is related to observations on injury location (for example, the head, while representing a small area of the whole body, tends to be a prime target for violent assaults) as much as injury morphology (bone breaks a certain way depending on the type of impact, such as a blow with a blunt object). This analytical process takes into consideration clinical, forensic, and experimental data as well as the skeleton's cultural context.[28] However, it may not always be possible to state with perfect certainty that an injury was violence-related; the more contextual and analytical detail is provided, the more secure the diagnosis.

Collated skeletal trauma data needs to be treated as a constrained resource when representing vastly different publication dates that reflect different research methods and often a diversity of research questions. Evidence of violent trauma might have been an incidental finding rather than the primary focus and might have been identified and diagnosed according to disparate criteria. Bioarchaeological analytical methods are constantly changing, and violent trauma analysis, in particular, has undergone a rapid progression over the last couple of decades.[29] Much of this comes back to the question of the coherence of the data set and the criteria for its selection, which in Pinker's case reflects a clear focus on English-language publications and their preselected ready availability. A growing body of recent work on violence-related trauma in the Neolithic has involved, in addition to new data on recently discovered sites, the reanalysis of existing assemblages according to current analytical protocols.[30] This has resulted in a more robust and more readily usable and comparable data set, one that keeps growing but has largely been ignored by Pinker.[31]

Another important consideration is the mixing of data from event-related sites—such as those resulting from one-off violent conflict or massacres like Crow Creek, a pre–European contact Native American site dating to 1325 CE that represents a large-scale violent event that might or might not be typical for the region and period—versus data from regular burial or cemetery sites, such as the earlier example of Mesolithic Vedbæk, which may be more indicative of the day-to-day level of violence within a society. These are discrete data sets on violent interaction that reflect rather different aspects of human behavior and society, for example, a large-scale massacre versus violent deaths within a community that might have resulted from a number of scenarios including one-to-one fighting, raiding, and revenge killings. These different data sets may also produce quite different injury and fatality patterns that can be closely related to age or gender and include or exclude whole sections of society.[32] This brings the argument back to criticisms of Pinker's figures. The issue here is not just simply with numerical values but with the lack of information on what parts of society these figures actually represent.

Conclusion

One could argue that many of the considerations and criticisms outlined above are addressing minor points of semantics that should not detract from the overarching thesis, but between the statistical and interdisciplinary shortcomings they do add up to a meaningful whole that should not be ignored. Despite affirmations to the contrary,[33] Pinker's account of prehistoric violence has neglected one of the most important aspects in this discussion, which is the significance of the experiential and contextual qualities of any violent event. Throughout the book, Pinker refers to the impression of living in an age of violence versus the actual degree of violence present and experienced, but he fails to critically examine this question for his own work on prehistory. How did people experience life in the distant past that was their daily present? We do not know whether the Mesolithic hunter-gatherer-fisher groups of Vedbæk viewed their lives as particularly violent, and with the still limited Mesolithic skeletal data set available we cannot say for certain how representative Vedbæk is of the wider European Mesolithic. Most importantly, though, reconciling comparisons of diverse types and scales of violence occurring in chronologically and socioculturally diverse contexts is more complex and challenging than Pinker suggests.

Archaeology's particularly close-up view of the past has always been inherently interdisciplinary, including the sciences and the humanities. Anybody who is borrowing from, appropriating, and ultimately "colonizing" related disciplines, or indeed the distant past, should avoid postcolonial attitudes. Like the attempt to understand the meaning and motivations behind past human actions, true interdisciplinarity can indeed be a foreign country when navigated without the support and guidance of those firmly rooted in the subjects we are trying to navigate.

Linda Fibiger is a Senior Lecturer in Human Osteoarchaeology at the University of Edinburgh and Programme Director of the MSc in Human Osteoarchaeology. She has published on the promotion of professional standards, ethics, and legislation in bioarchaeology, and is currently involved in the ERC-funded The Fall of 1200 BC *project which investigates the role of migration and conflict in social crises at the end of the Bronze Age in South-Eastern Europe.*

Notes

1. Steven Pinker, *The Better Angels of Our Nature* (New York: Viking, 2011).
2. Lawrence H. Keeley, *War Before Civilization: The Myth of the Peaceful Savage* (Oxford: Oxford University Press, 1996).
3. Pasquale Cirillo and Nassim N. Taleb, "On the Statistical Properties and Tail Risk of Violent Conflicts," *Physica A: Statistical Mechanics and its Applications* 452 (2016): 29–45; Dean Falk and Charles Hildebolt, "Annual War Deaths in Small-Scale

versus State Societies Scale with Population Size Rather than Violence," *Current Anthropology* 58, no. 6 (2017): 805–813.

4. Rahul C. Oka, Marc Kissel, Mark Golitko, Susan Guise Sheridan, Nam C. Kim, and Agustín Fuentes, "Population is the Main Driver of War Group Size and Conflict Casualties," *Proceedings of the National Academy of Sciences*, 114, no. 52 (2017): E11101–E11110.

5. World Archaeological Congress, "The Vermillion Accord," http://worldarch.org/code-of-ethics/ (accessed 20 November 2017).

6. Pinker, *Better Angels*, xxiv.

7. Chris Scarre, ed., *The Human Past: World Prehistory and the Development of Human Societies*, 2nd ed. (London: Thames & Hudson, 2009).

8. Pinker, *Better Angels*, 49.

9. Mike P. Richards, T. Douglas Price, and Eva Koch, "Mesolithic and Neolithic Subsistence in Denmark: New Stable Isotope Data," *Current Anthropology* 44, no. 2 (2006): 288–295.

10. John Robb, "Violence and Gender in Early Italy," in *Troubled Times: Violence and Warfare in the Past*, ed. Debra L. Martin and David W. Frayer (Amsterdam: Gordon & Breach, 1997), 111–144; Philip L. Walker, "A Bioarchaeological Perspective on the History of Violence," *Annual Review of Anthropology* 30, no. 1 (2001): 573–596.

11. Göran Aijmer, "Introduction: The Idiom of Violence in Imagery and Discourse," in *Meanings of Violence: A Cross Cultural Perspective*, ed. Göran Aijmer and Jon Abbink (Oxford: Berg, 2000), 1–21; Quincy Wright, "Definitions of War," in *War*, ed. Lawrence Freedman (Oxford: Oxford University Press, 1994), 69–70; R. Brian Ferguson, "Introduction: Studying War," in *Warfare, Culture and Environment*, ed. R. Brian Ferguson (Orlando: Academic Press, 1984), 1–81.

12. Joshua S. Goldstein, *War and Gender* (Cambridge: Cambridge University Press, 2001); Carol R. Ember and Melvin Ember, "War, Socialization, and Interpersonal Violence: A Cross-Cultural Study," *Journal of Conflict Resolution* 38, no. 4 (1994): 620–646; James R. Kerin, "Combat," in *Encyclopedia of Violence, Peace and Conflict*, ed. Lester R. Kurtz, 2nd ed. (San Diego: Academic Press, 1998), 349.

13. David Warbourton, "Aspects of War and Warfare in Western Philosophy and History," in *Warfare and Society: Archaeological and Social Anthropological Perspectives*, ed. Ton Otto, Henrik Thrane, and Helle Vandkilde (Aarhus: Aarhus University Press, 2006), 37–55.

14. Robert O'Connell, *Ride of the Second Horseman: The Birth and Death of War* (Oxford: Gordon & Breach, 1995).

15. Herbert D. G. Maschner and Katherine L. Reedy-Maschner, "Raid, Retreat, Defend (Repeat): The Archaeology and Ethnohistory of Warfare on the North Pacific Rim," *Journal of Anthropological Archaeology* 17, no. 1 (1998): 19–51.

16. Donald F. Tuzin, "The Spectre of Peace in Unlikely Places: Concept and Paradox in the Anthropology of Peace," in *A Natural History of Peace*, ed. Thomas Gregor (Nashville: Vanderbilt University Press, 1996), 3–33; Patrick S. Willey, *Prehistoric Warfare on the Great Plains: Skeletal Analysis of the Crow Creek Massacre Victims* (New York: Garland, 1990).

17. Robert K. Dentan, "Recent Studies on Violence: What's In and What's Out," *Reviews in Anthropology* 37, no. 1 (2008): 41–67.

18. John Sharp, "Tribe," in *The Social Science Encyclopedia*, ed. Adam Kuper and Jessica Kuper (London: Routledge, 1996), 857–859; Aiden Southall, "Tribes," in

Encyclopedia of Cultural Anthropology, ed. David Levinson and Melvin Ember (New York: Henry Holt & Company, 1996), 1332; Morton Fried, *The Evolution of Political Society* (New York: Random House, 1967).

19. Jürg Helbling, "War and Peace in Societies without Central Power," in *Warfare and Society: Archaeological and Social Anthropological Perspectives,* ed. Ton Otto, Henrik Thrane, and Helle Vandkilde (Aarhus: Aarhus University Press, 2006), 113–139; Jonathan Haas, "Warfare and the Evolution of Tribal Polities in the Prehistoric Southwest," in *The Anthropology of War,* ed. Jonathan Haas (Cambridge: Cambridge University Press, 1990), 171–189.

20. Wolfgang Haak, Guido Brandt, Hylke N. de Jong, Christian Meyer, Robert Ganslmeier, Volker Heyd, Chris Hawkesworth, Alistair W. G. Pike, Harald Meller, and Kurt W. Alt, "Ancient DNA, Strontium Isotopes, and Osteological Analyses Shed Light on Social and Kinship Organization of the Later Stone Age," *Proceedings of the National Academy of Sciences* 105, no. 2 (2008): 18226–18231.

21. Emanuel Marx, "The Tribe as a Unit of Subsistence: Nomadic Pastoralism in the Middle East," *American Anthropologist* 79, no. 2 (1977): 343–363.

22. Nicholas Márquez-Grant, Hannah Webster, Janamarie Truesdell, and Linda Fibiger, "Physical Anthropology and Osteoarchaeology in Europe: History, Current Trends and Challenges," *International Journal of Osteoarchaeology* 26, no. 6 (2016): 1078–1088.

23. Pinker, *Better Angels,* 48.

24. Ibid., 51.

25. R. Brian Ferguson, "Pinker's List," in *War, Peace, and Human Nature: The Convergence of Evolutionary and Cultural Views,* ed. Douglas P. Fry (Oxford: Oxford University Press, 2013), 112–131; R. Brian Ferguson, "The Prehistory of War and Peace in Europe and the Near East," in *War, Peace, and Human Nature,* 191–240.

26. Joachim Wahl and H. G. König, "Anthropologisch-traumatologische Untersuchung der Menschlichen Skelettreste aus dem Bandkeramischen Massengrab bei Talheim, Kreis Heilbronn," *Fundberichte aus Baden-Württemberg* 12 (1987): 65–193.

27. Linda Fibiger, Torbjörn Ahlström, Pia Bennike, and Rick J. Schulting, "Patterns of Violence-Related Skull Trauma in Neolithic Southern Scandinavia," *American Journal of Physical Anthropology* 150 (2013): 190–202; Pia Bennike, *Palaeopathology of Danish Skeletons* (Copenhagen: Akademisk Forlag, 1985).

28. Fibiger et al., "Patterns of Violence-Related Skull Trauma in Neolithic Southern Scandinavia"; Meaghan Dyer and Linda Fibiger, "Understanding Blunt Force Trauma and Violence in Neolithic Europe: The First Experiments Using a Skin-Skull-Brain Model and the Thames Beater," *Antiquity* 91, no. 360 (2017): 1515–1528.

29. Vicki L. Wedel and Allison Galloway, *Broken Bones: Anthropological Analysis of Blunt Force Trauma,* 2nd ed. (Springfield, IL: Charles C. Thomas, 2014).

30. Rick Schulting and Mike Wysocki, "In This Chambered Tomb Were Found Cleft Skulls . . .": An Assessment of the Evidence for Cranial Trauma in the British Neolithic," *Proceedings of the Prehistoric Society* 71 (2005): 107–138; Martin Smith and Megan Brickley, *People of the Long Barrows: Life, Death and Burial in the Earlier Neolithic* (Stroud: History Press, 2009), 102–112.

31. *The Routledge Handbook of the Bioarchaeology of Human Conflict,* ed. Chris Knüsel and Martin Smith (Abingdon, UK: Routledge, 2014).

32. Linda Fibiger, "Misplaced Childhood? Interpersonal Violence and Children in Neolithic Europe," in Knüsel and Smith, *The Routledge Handbook of the Bioarchaeology of Human Conflict,* 27–145.
33. Pinker, *Better Angels,* 696.

Chapter 2

Were There Better Angels of a Classical Greek Nature?
Violence in Classical Athens

Matthew Trundle

S teven Pinker discusses ancient Greek civilization only briefly at the beginning of his work, and simply to highlight the violence of heroes such
as Achilles and Odysseus depicted in the Homeric poems. How do Pinker's
ideas relate to violence in classical Athens? He argues that a "civilizing process," alongside the rise of the modern nation-state that holds a monopoly
on force, has led to a decline of violence.[1] He adds that the growing significance of commerce and technologies have facilitated trade and intercon-
nectedness. He notes the increasingly significant role of women in society
alongside a cosmopolitanism, connected to the rise of globalism, literacy, and
the new media. Finally, he hails the triumph of reason, which has heralded
a growth in knowledge and empathy. Some modern notions do not apply to
antiquity. Universal human rights were largely absent, elite men dominated
everywhere, and slavery was normal. The ancient world was complex, however, with robust political states, long-distance trade, and a cultural inter-
connectivity across much of the eastern Mediterranean. The growing role of
the Athenian state in the Greek world as the sole arbiter of violence between
individuals and communities provides a useful connection to Pinker's ideas.
Pinker and antiquity have much to tell each other.

Pinker promotes the notion that the present is better than the past. Despite some early thinkers who saw progress in Christianity (for example, Augustine of Hippo) or early modern philosophers like Francis Bacon who noted improvements to the state of human kind, this is essentially a recent, post-Enlightenment and postindustrialization development. Ancient peoples believed in the intrinsic good of the past. For them, their ancient past was a better place than their present. Notions of progress or improvement were largely alien to ancient Greeks.[2] The distant past was a golden age in which the gods lived in harmony with nature. This was true as much for the Romans and the Hebrews as it was for the Greeks. The earliest Greek poets, Homer and Hesiod, who together laid the foundations for understanding the pantheon of Greek gods and creating the mythologies of the origins of the world, both present this view of the past. To Hesiod, the golden age gave way to silver and silver to bronze, each one a lesser age than the one it replaced.[3] The bronze age was the age of heroes like Herakles and Achilles and of events like the Trojan War. Hesiod lived in an iron age, one of hard living conditions and poverty.[4] We see similar notions in the Bible, in which the expulsion from the Garden of Eden represented a turning point for the worse in the affairs of human beings.[5] Ancient ideology frequently promoted the "good old days" of the past over the present.

Such notions can be seen in views of violence and its role in the ancient past, and warfare presents a paradigm. Our sources present a vision of the past as one of "fair play" and rules-based wars.[6] Early Greek military encounters smack of the amateur and unprofessional.[7] We might see in such thinking parallels with modern notions of sport—once the domain of the amateur gentlemen, but now entirely professionalized. Winning and money have become the only currencies, rather than amateur glory and honor, to the detriment of the game itself.[8] Homer's poems present an image of an older and idealized world behind its already old and idealized epic story. The aged Nestor claims there were no specialists to compete at athletic games when he was young, just gifted all-rounders.[9] This was surely a dig at the specializing tendency of Greek athletic contests and by implication warfare.

Our ancient sources consistently state this "good old days" view of the past. Demosthenes in the 340s BCE writes that in the past fighting was fair and open, conducted on a prescribed day and time, but in his present battles are fought year-round with the Macedonian Philip (father of Alexander the Great) using guile and cheating to win wars.[10] Two hundred years later Polybius mirrors the same message in exactly the same way. His villain of the piece is another Macedonian ruler, Philip V, active in the late third and early second century BCE, who cheats his way to victory.[11] Both writers emphasize the justness of open and honest war making.

This ideology of fairness in warfare included both an aristocratic belief in the absolute good of heavy infantry hand-to-hand fighting, and a consequent prejudice against missile weapons, slings, bows, and javelins.[12] Ancient Greek society closely associated landowning farmers and service as heavy infantrymen. Missile weapons were effective, but they were cheaper than armor and could kill anyone without warning. Despite notable heroes who were skilled archers (like Odysseus, Teucer, or Paris), Homer illustrates the stigma against those who shot arrows from afar rather than fighting toe to toe with shield and spear. Diomedes calls Paris a "girl," a "silly boy," and a "worthless coward" for shooting an arrow, "which only grazed him."[13] The Greek historical record provides plenty of hostility to missile weapons. A treaty concerning the supposed and largely mythical Lelantine War of the later eighth century BCE forbade long-distance missiles in the conflict.[14] Thucydides laments the deaths of hoplites in Aetolia and Sphacteria at the hands of light infantry.[15] Xenophon mirrors the same sentiment when eulogizing the dead at Lechaeum.[16] Greek aristocratic hostility to light armed troops resembles the prejudice of medieval elites against longbowmen who could bring down an armored knight from a hundred yards or more. Our sources present the prejudice in terms of justness. Despite this, missiles remained an integral part of warfare throughout antiquity. Pinker's thesis applies in the way moderns might see attitudes to the myth and the reality of warfare and violence, as well as to notions of justice in warfare in the past.

The growing role of the state in all aspects of people's lives is a crucial linchpin that links Pinker's ideas to those of antiquity. The perception of a changing world outlined in my long introduction, whereby the ancient Greeks saw the past in idealized terms and their own age as somehow lesser and harsher, certainly has some truth as it relates to the growing political significance of the state. It is easy to see that wars grew greater and more centralized as the power of states grew. At the same time the power of the individual aristocracies declined. Violence became the domain of the political community and wars changed exponentially as a result.

Victor Davis Hanson has led a school of thought that early Greek wars in the Archaic period were regulated and almost ritualized affairs.[17] Greek states fought limited and short wars through a single battle at an agreed time and place in which heavily armed soldiers who were primarily amateur-farmers fought over marginal land at the edge of Greek poleis. The battle was decided by a single and brief clash of arms. The losers fled, discarding their shields and armor, while the victors held the field. Pursuit was limited and therefore neither losers nor victors lost many men in the encounter. This thesis reflects the statements of Demosthenes and Polybius of a "good old days" in which earlier wars were less destructive and more civilized. It also hints at war as sport rather than a serious and devastating experience. Hanson argued that the idea of a pitched battle, decisive in its outcome but limited in its overall damage, was foundational in what he styled as the "western way of war." This way of fighting, he argued, was somehow different from eastern warfare, which was (and by implication is) deceitful and guerrilla-style in its nature.

Despite the fact that there is limited evidence for how Greeks actually fought their wars in the Archaic period, and the romanticism about war as a game, some evidence supports Hanson's thesis. There might well have been an *agônal* (or ritualized struggle) aspect to early military encounters. Supposed ritualized hoplite battles of the early ancient Greek past, rule-based *agônal* struggles, gave way to larger and more aggressive wars in the classical period. Thucydides sketches these changes and the development of military capability linked to the growing power, wealth, and centralization of Greek states in the fifth century BCE.[18] The centralization of the state as a key protagonist for changes in warfare in the sixth and fifth centuries BCE links neatly to Pinker's argument that the state has become the arbiter and controller of violence in the modern world. Athenian centralization led to larger and more sophisticated navies, especially thanks to state money.[19] Thus, wars grew in size in the Greek world, as well as in complexity and destructiveness.[20] This appears to be valid for land wars as well as those at sea. Wars in the later fifth century were indeed bigger and more devastating, especially if compared to Herodotus's admittedly sketchy vision of early Greek land battles, which suggests that wars prior to the Persian invasion were indeed smaller and more limited military engagements.

More recently than Hanson, J. E. Lendon argued that the past hung heavily on later Greek (and Roman) soldiers in their attitudes to warfare and shaped the way that Homer's heroic descendants fought their battles.[21] In *Soldiers and Ghosts* he suggests that tradition not only informed the future, but also both influenced and constrained it. In his view, the aristocratic, heroic, and glorious nature of earlier military participants were used as paradigms to dictate military developments. Strategists looked back to Homer for precedents in a strange and cyclical "back to the future" ideology in order to introduce new battlefield technologies.

There is little doubt that ancient Greek wars grew in magnitude over time. We can chart dimensional changes both in numbers of combatants and the size of victory-to-defeat ratios from the sixth to the fourth century BCE in the Greek world. The evidence that we have for Archaic battles suggests that outcomes were regulated and limited in degree. Herodotus records several battles of "Champions" in which small numbers of selected and elite representatives fought battles on behalf of their communities.[22] Herodotus also records stories that are abominations against the norms of the day. Cleomenes shocked the Greek world when he burned to death six thousand Argives in a sacred grove.[23] The story was no doubt shocking not only because of the numbers of dead but also because of the rule-breaking desecration of the grove itself. The Athenian victory at Marathon saw 6,400 Persian dead, a huge number for the time.[24] Battlefield losses in the early fifth century were relatively low.[25] Over time, numbers of dead on battlefields grew along with improved tactics and more specialist forces. Alexander's victory at Gaugamela in 331 BCE saw his 50,000 men defeat a Persian force of several hundred thousand and kill some 100,000 in a day.[26] The Battle of Ipsus in 301 BCE saw Antigonus's 70,000 professional soldiers defeated by Seleucus's 80,000.[27] The losses inflicted on defeated opponents grew as war became more effective over time. In this sense, later classical Greeks could be forgiven for thinking that they lived in a more violent world.

Thucydides noted that navies and siege technology had developed in the classical age to facilitate total war. More technologically advanced vessels, like the *trierês* (three) or trireme, with three banks of oars one above the other and 180 oarsmen, superseded early Greek ships, so-called fifties that held 50 oars on a single level.[28] Navies from the later sixth century BCE required thousands of rowers. Larger quad- and quinqueremes, fours and fives, invented in the fourth century, replaced the smaller triremes. Some quinqueremes had crews of about three hundred men. Siege technology developed in tandem with naval developments.[29] These came from the east, primarily from the Assyrians, who led the world in siege machines like rams, towers, and catapults. Polybius rightly saw wars in his own day as larger than those of the past, and he too identified technological developments as part of a teleological process resulting in bigger and more devastating wars. In his day Rome had followed Alexander's lead to conquer the "known" world.

Ancient peoples became better at warfare as their communities coalesced and resources centralized. They developed better mechanisms to destroy their enemies in land battles, sieges, and at sea. Thucydides (as Polybius did later) noted this process. In the past, he says, wars were smaller and took longer because of lack of *chrêmata* or resources.[30] By his day what he meant by *chrêmata* was coined money. Troy, he says, would have fallen more quickly if the men had not had to spend so much time looking for provisions or farming the land to survive during the siege. If they had had money, they could have concentrated on prosecuting the siege itself. Thanks to money, armies in the field could provision themselves by selling booty for coins and using money to pay for food rather than foraging for it in the field. Money centralized the military process, making wars more efficient. Wars had become bigger and nastier because of the abilities of states to coordinate their resources and develop better military technologies, not because people had become nastier or more aggressive.[31] War in whatever form is never a game and there never was a "good old days," despite what aristocratic ideology (both ancient and modern) might suggest.

Paradoxes in ancient thinking about the supposed good old days did, of course, exist. The Trojan War ended in terrible destruction. The rules of war were broken in the sack of the city, the murder of suppliants in temples and at altars, the killing of innocent children, and the wholesale enslavement of the survivors. Even the taking of the city transgressed rules of fair play. The wooden horse represents the paradigm of a device designed to deceive the enemy. The fact that the horse was dressed up as a gift to the god Poseidon added religious insult to injury. Siege machines, rams, tunnels, towers, and ballista were called by the Greeks *mêchanai*—which itself was a word that had connotations of deception and unfairness. The "machine" was more than a feat of engineering, but a contrivance. Troy was a foundational struggle for later Greeks who strove to claim descent from both sides. Nothing like the ten-year siege and sack of the city had been witnessed in the Greek world for centuries after the fall of Troy. Walled cities appeared commonly in the Aegean only in the later Archaic period, after about 600 BCE. Sieges in which Greeks took cities by storm were unknown before the late fifth century BCE. In these regards the Greeks lagged far behind their Near Eastern neighbors. Cities were reduced by circumvallation, blockade, and starvation—as occurred to Athenian rivals such as Naxos, Thasos, Samos, and Mytilene—rather than by storm.[32] The siege of Syracuse similarly saw the Athenians attempt and fail to isolate the town, which resulted in their own defeat.[33]

The changes that Greeks perceived over time were technological rather than attitudinal. There never was a "good old days" in the sense of fair play. It was not because earlier Greeks played fairer or thought it unsporting to fight wars less openly or let the enemy escape battlefields, but simply because they lacked the technology, the military wherewithal, to destroy the enemy in toto. The introduction of varied specialist infantry and cavalry enabled commanders to develop better tactics and to pursue the defeated army off the field of battle. In this way, the Pinker Thesis regarding ancient military capabilities is right in the sense that states command power and centralized resources to wage war more effectively, but arguably wrong in the sense that this reduced the likelihood of violent destruction.

Of some relevance to the Pinker Thesis, we might consider the relationship between different forms of government and violence. Ancient philosophers identified three basic forms of government in antiquity—monarchy, aristocracy, and democracy—each of which had less benign manifestations in the forms of tyranny, oligarchy and ochlocracy, or mob rule.[34] There was certainly a theme among ancient aristocratic writers that monarchies and aristocracies tended to shun overseas wars. John Keane recently asked the question, "Does democracy have a violent heart?"[35] He explores the Athenian imperial moment and notions of the democratization of war connected to imperial Athens.[36] The Athenian democracy became increasingly violent through the fifth century both with regard to the treatment of its subject-allies and its interest in overseas conquest. Radical democracy and imperial violence became closely associated.

War in Athens was a democratic phenomenon. The assembly voted for war or peace and many then participated in military actions that followed. Even before the empire the assembly of the new democracy appears greedy for riches plundered from abroad. Athenians voted to help the Ionian revolt, persuaded by the lure of easy wealth in the east.[37] They funded Miltiades on a mission he claimed would bring them gold.[38] Thucydides and other aristocrats criticized Athenian decisions based on the greed of the poor, who made up a majority in the assembly. Athenian leadership, itself the result of democratic support, led the state into more aggressive actions as the Peloponnesian War progressed. Thucydides describes Cleon, who had replaced Pericles as the people's leader, as the most violent (*biaiotatos*) of men.[39] Cleon was an out-and-out imperialist. Thucydides claims the poor voted to attack Sicily in hopes of years of wage earning (*misthophoria*) from conquest.[40] Warfare, particularly at sea, required increasing numbers of participants and consumed enormous resources. War and imperialism became means of revenue extraction. Athens had become trapped in a vicious cycle of expenditure and acquisition to fuel its wars and grow its empire. State control of violence for Athens meant greater harm for other states.

If we turn our attention away from foreign policy and war making to levels of everyday violence within Athens, can we draw from the Pinker Thesis notions of improvement over time? To Pinker, social relationships within communities are today less violent than they were in the past. Here he may well have a point. The ancient world remained a violent place within communities. The ancient world saw no empowerment of women and probably no enhanced powers of reasoning and expanding capacities for empathy that might occur in some modern environments. "Low-level violence," a label coined to cover instances of violence that did not involve the levying of a state's resources for mass military purposes, was an everyday phenomenon throughout all ancient society.[41] Athens was no exception.[42] Violence enforced power relationships and indeed mediated social encounters.[43] Men beat women, masters beat slaves, and corporal and capital punishments, some brutal like the *tumpanismos* (crucifixion), were commonplace. Women were regularly victims of sexual violence even in the high classical period.

A degree of amelioration regarding violence, however, did occur in certain ways. Homer records how Odysseus beat the unruly and lowly Thersites in the assembly, suggestive of arcane power relationships.[44] Citizens in most classical states were prohibited from beating fellow citizens. Thucydides noted that some Greeks from outside Athens still carried arms in public places in his own day, unlike his own city, where such practice was no longer the case. The Athenians had come to adopt a more peaceful way of life.[45] Were fifth-century Athenians more peaceful than their neighbors and predecessors? Were they indeed forerunners of Pinker's modern world? Gabriel Herman wrote that Athenian society "must be classed among the less violent societies of preindustrial Europe."[46] He identifies four key reasons for this: (1) unarmed citizens, (2) a nonmilitant ideology, (3) the absence of a culture based on vendetta and blood feud, and (4) the Athenian judicial system. Our assessment can be only relative, however, and in some regards it is all about perspective. Some argue that the Athenian judicial system was a paragon of legal control of bad behavior, while others see it simply as an extension of family feuding and violence.[47] Self-help, or state-sanctioned vigilantism, remained essential aspects of the Athenian legal process. In the absence of a state prosecution service, a genuine state police force, and criminal investigation department to investigate crimes or enforce verdicts, it is hard to praise Athenian progressive legal developments too loudly in modern Western terms.

Plenty of evidence suggests that violence still plagued Greek poleis in the later fifth century BCE. Democracy did not necessarily herald a community approach to promote legal equality or to suppress individual aggression within the state. Athenian democrats used violence as often as their oligarchic enemies in fighting their political opponents.[48] Thucydides's *Histories* are full of lessons to be learned from the breakdown of society in the extreme moments of warfare and political strife. None were more extreme than the wars of the later fifth century BCE, and Thucydides paints a grim picture of political stasis and the violence that it entailed within many Greek communities. The Corcyraean civil war between democrats and oligarchs and similar revolutions across the Greek cities and the effects these had on human nature and society more generally reveal the chaos that might ensue with sociopolitical upheaval. In an oft-quoted passage, Thucydides notes how in peace and prosperity states and individuals behave better, but war creates different realities. Violence is a product of circumstance.[49] There could be no better commentary on the relationship between civilization and peace, on the one hand, and war and dystopia, on the other.

One of the problems with assessing the value of theories like those of Pinker in understanding the past is that we can see more than simple snapshots of time in a long period like antiquity. Even if we were to accept Pinker's thesis for the world in which we currently live, we have no way of knowing that we will continue to live as settled and as peaceful lives as he suggests in Western countries, in both relative and absolute terms. Athenians created a centralized and relatively cohesive state in the middle of the fifth century built around their democratic principles and also their empire, but later events saw their society break down into moments of political and violent oligarchic revolution in 411 and 404–403 BCE. The fourth century BCE saw a series of wars for hegemony plague the Greek world before the final conquests of Philip II of Macedon and his son Alexander the Great transformed the eastern Mediterranean.

In conclusion, Pinker is correct to see the importance of the state as the arbiter and controlling agent of violence. In antiquity, however, the state, far from being a means to curb violent activity, actually promoted it. States like Athens could apply maximum force and power against their neighbors in a world with different international rules and regulations than ours. More significantly, and more supportive of the Pinker Thesis, an ancient state's "government" (that is, the elite) did not extend its protection to all who lived within its boundaries. Even wealthy citizens had to defend themselves against the actions of others, let alone the disenfranchised slaves, foreign residents, and even women who were relatives of citizens within the state. Violence in any form is still violence—even so-called low-level violence. In antiquity, such violence was common, tolerated, and sanctioned. In this regard Pinker's thesis has a crucial point. Low-level violence might be ubiquitous in modern states, but modern states, their legal systems, and above all public opinion no longer (theoretically) tolerate, let alone sanction, low-level violence at all.

Acknowledgments

I would like to thank my colleagues Dr. Jeremy Armstrong (University of Auckland), Dr. Jason Crowley (Manchester Metropolitan University), and Dr. Bob Tristram for invaluable comments on earlier drafts of this essay. All errors are my own.

Matthew Trundle was Chair and Professor of Classics and Ancient History at the University of Auckland, New Zealand. His research interests were primarily in ancient Greek history and society. He was one of the editors of the Cambridge World History of Violence.

Notes

1. Steven Pinker, *The Better Angels of Our Nature: Why Violence Has Declined* (London: Penguin, 2011).
2. On ancient attitudes toward progress, see Eric Robertson Dodds, "The Ancient Concept of Progress," in *The Ancient Concept of Progress and other Essays on Greek Literature and Belief*, ed. E. R. Dodds (Oxford: Clarendon Press, 1973), 1–25; Serafina Cuomo, *Technology and Culture in Greek and Roman Antiquity* (Cambridge: Cambridge University Press, 2007).
3. Hesiod, *Works and Days,* 109–174. In this and all other references to ancient literary works, translations are the author's own. Refer to the Loeb Classical Library editions for line references.
4. Ibid., 175–184.
5. Genesis 3:6–24.
6. The lie is best put to this notion by Peter Krentz, "Fighting by the Rules: The Invention of the Hoplite *Agôn*," *Hesperia* 71 (1982): 23–39; more optimistically, see Josiah Ober, "The Rules of War in Classical Greece," in *The Athenian Revolution,* ed. Josiah Ober (Princeton, NJ: Princeton University Press, 1998), 53–71.
7. For a good discussion of early Greek warfare and the potential changes that took place over time, see Matthew Lloyd, "Unorthodox Warfare? Variety and Change in Archaic Greek Warfare (ca. 700–ca. 480 BCE)," in *Unconventional Warfare from Antiquity to the Present Day,* ed. B. Hughes and F. Robson (Oxford: Oxford University Press, 2017), 231–252; Hans van Wees, *Greek Warfare: Myths and Realities* (London: Duckworth, 2004), 95–97, 153–165; Louis Rawlings, *The Ancient Greeks at War* (Manchester: Manchester University Press, 2007), 19–42; P. A. L. Greenhalgh, *Early Greek Warfare* (Cambridge: Cambridge University Press, 1973); Alistair Jackson, "Wars and Raids for Booty in the World of Odysseus," in *War and Society in the Greek World,* ed. John Rich and Graham Shipley (London: Routledge, 1993), 64–76; Victor Davis Hanson, *Warfare and Agriculture in Ancient Greece* (Pisa: Giardini, 1983), esp. chap. 6.
8. For discussion and bibliography of the relationship between war and sport in the Greek world, see Matthew Trundle, "Greek Athletes and Warfare in the Classical Period," *Nikephoros: Zeitschrift für Sport und Kultur im Altertum* 25 (2012 [published 2014]): 221–237; David Pritchard, ed., *War, Democracy and Culture in Classical Athens* (Cambridge: Cambridge University Press, 2013).

9. Homer, *Iliad* 23.695–719.
10. Demosthenes 9.47–50.
11. Polybius, *Histories* 13.3.28.
12. On light troops in classical antiquity, see most recently David Pritchard, "The Archers of Classical Athens," *Greece and Rome* 65 (2018): 1–16; Matthew Trundle, "Light Armed Troops in Classical Athens," in Pritchard, *War, Democracy and Culture,* 139–160.
13. *Iliad* 11.384–395.
14. Archilochus, frag. 3; Strabo 10.1.2.
15. Thucydides 3.98.3 and 4.40.
16. Xenophon, *Hellenica* 4.5.11–18; Plutarch, *Agesilaus* 22.2.
17. Victor Davis Hanson, *The Western Way of War: Infantry Battle in Classical Greece* (Los Angeles: University of California Press, 1979); Victor Davis Hanson, *The Other Greeks: The Family Farm and the Roots of Western Civilization* (New York: Free Press, 1995). More recently this has been asserted by Adam Schwartz, *Reinstating the Hoplite: Arms, Armour and Phalanx Fighting in Archaic and Classical Greece* (Stuttgart: Franz Steiner Verlag, 2010). The ritualized nature of hoplite combat is well discussed by Walter Garrison Runciman, "Greek Hoplites, Warrior Culture, and Indirect Bias," *Journal of the Royal Anthropological Institute* 4, no. 4 (1998): 731–751.
18. Thucydides 1.10–13.
19. Ibid. 1.13–16.
20. Ibid. 1.13.
21. John Edward Lendon, *Soldiers and Ghosts: A History of Battle in Antiquity* (New Haven, CT: Yale University Press, 2005).
22. For example, see Herodotus 1.82 (The Battle of the Champions), Thermopylae (7.207–234), 9.64 (Stenyclerus); Thucydides (5.41) notes that a clause in a treaty between Argos and Sparta provided for dispute to be settled by such champions as had happened in the past.
23. Herodotus 6.79–80.
24. Ibid. 6.117.1.
25. See Adam Schwartz, *Reinstating the Hoplite,* from page 292 for a comprehensive "Battle Inventory" of military encounters including, where we know them, casualty figures.
26. Arrian, *Anabasis* 3.7–15; Diodorus 17.53–61; Plutarch, *Alexander* 31–34.
27. Plutarch, *Demetrius* 28–29.
28. On the rise of the trireme, see Wees, *Greek Warfare,* 206–231; John S. Morrison, John F. Coates, and N. Boris Rankov, *The Athenian Trireme* (Cambridge: Cambridge University Press, 2000), 34–46; Herman T. Wallinga, *Ships and Sea-Power Before the Persian War* (Leiden: Brill, 1993), 103–129; Lionel Casson, *The Ancient Mariners* (Princeton, NJ: Princeton University Press, 1991), 83–96. For discussion of the role of coinage in naval developments in the later sixth century and possible associations toward trireme adoption, see Hans van Wees, "Those Who Sail Shall Receive a Wage," in *New Perspectives on Ancient Warfare,* ed. Garrett Fagan and Matthew Trundle (Leiden: Brill, 2010), 205–225. For an emphasis on early developments, see Christopher Haas, "Athenian Naval Power Before Themistocles," *Historia* 34 (1985): 29–46; Philip de Souza, "Towards Thalassocracy: Archaic Greek Naval Developments," in *Archaic Greece: New Approaches and Developments,* ed. N. Fisher and Hans van Wees (London: Duckworth, 1998), 271–294.

29. For good introductions and overview, see Barry Strauss, "Naval Battles and Sieges," in *The Cambridge History of Greek and Roman Warfare*, ed. Philip Sabin, Hans van Wees, and Michael Whitby (Cambridge: Cambridge University Press, 2008), 223–247; Louis Rawlings, *Greek Warfare*, 132–140; Wees, *Greek Warfare*, 136–144.

30. Thucydides 1.11.1.

31. For further discussion and bibliography, see Matthew Trundle, "Coinage and the Transformation of Greek Warfare," in Fagan and Trundle, *New Perspectives*, 227–252.

32. Naxos (Thucydides 1.98), Thasos (Thucydides 1.101), Samos (Thucydides 1.117.3), and Mytilene (Thucydides 3.27).

33. Thucydides books 6 and 7.

34. Aristotle, *Politics* 1279a32; and see 1279b11–1280a6.

35. John Keane, "Does Democracy Have a Violent Heart?," in Pritchard, *War, Democracy and Culture*, 378–408.

36. Ibid., 381–384. For the economics of Athenian imperialism, see most recently Matthew Trundle, "Coinage and the Economics of the Athenian Empire," in *Circum Mare: Themes in Ancient Warfare*, ed. Jeremy Armstrong (Leiden: Brill, 2016), 65–79.

37. Herodotus 5.97.

38. Ibid. 6.132.

39. Thucydides 3.36.6.

40. Ibid. 6.24.1–4; see also 6.46.3–5.

41. For example, in classical Athens, see Jason Crowley, *The Psychology of the Athenian Hoplite* (Cambridge: Cambridge University Press, 2013), 93; Edward Cohen, *The Athenian Nation* (Princeton, NJ: Princeton University Press, 2005), 176. On violence, most recently and across several spectrums of the classical world, see Werner Riess and Garrett Fagan, eds., *The Topography of Violence in the Greco-Roman World* (Ann Arbor: University of Michigan Press, 2016); especially for Athenian culture see Riess's own chapter, "Where to Kill in Classical Athens," 77–104.

42. See Werner Riess, *Performing Interpersonal Violence: Court, Curse, and Comedy in Fourth Century BCE Athens* (Berlin: De Gruyter, 2012).

43. For good recent discussion, see Rosanna Omitowoju, "The Crime That Dare Not Speak Its Name: Violence Against Women in the Athenian Courts," in Riess and Fagan, *Topography*, 113–135; Peter Hunt, "Violence Against Slaves in Classical Greece," in Riess and Fagan, *Topography*, 137–161. For sexual violence against women, see, especially, Rosanna Omitowoju, *Rape and the Politics of Consent in Classical Athens* (Cambridge: Cambridge University Press, 2002).

44. Homer, *Iliad* 2.246.

45. Thucydides, 1.5.3–6.1, 1.6.2; see also Hans van Wees, "Greeks Bearing Arms: State, the Leisure Class and the Display of Weapons in Ancient Greece," in *Archaic Greece: New Approaches and New Evidence*, ed. Nicholas Fisher and H. van Wees (London: Routledge, 1998), 333–378; Gabriel Herman, *Morality and Behavior in Democratic Athens: A Social History* (Cambridge: Cambridge University Press, 2006), 206–215.

46. Gabriel Herman, "How Violent was Athenian Society?," in *Ritual, Finance, Politics: Athenian Democratic Accounts Presented to David Lewis—the History and Archaeology of Athenian Democracy*, ed. Robin Osborne and Simon Hornblower (Oxford: Oxford University Press, 1993), 99–117.

47. For discussions, see Herman, "How Violent?," 99–117; Edward Harris, "Feuding or the Rule of Law? The Nature of Litigation in Classical Athens—an Essay in Legal Sociology," in *Symopsium 2001: Vortrage zue griechischen und hellenistischen Rechtsgeschichte,* ed. Robert Wallace and Michael Gagarin (Vienna: Franz Steiner Verlag, 2005), 125–141; Edward Cohen, *Law, Violence and Community in Classical Athens* (Cambridge: Cambridge University Press, 1995); Sally Humphreys, "Law as Discourse," in *Special Edition of History and Anthropology* 1, no. 2 (1985): 241–264.
48. Thucydides 8.90–92; Lysias 13.70–72; Lycurgus 1.112–115; *IG1*(3) 102; for discussion, see Riess, *Performing Interpersonal Violence,* 41, 52–53; Riess, "Where to Kill in Classical Athens."
49. Thucydides 3.82.2.

Chapter 3

Getting Medieval on Steven Pinker
Violence and Medieval England

Sara M. Butler

In *The Better Angels of Our Nature,* Steven Pinker puts forward a vision of the Middle Ages that is both grim and fearsome. He writes that "medieval Christendom was a culture of cruelty" in which "brutality" was "woven into the fabric of daily existence."[1] In a sketch from *Das Mittelalterliche Hausbuch* (The medieval housebook) depicting what Pinker describes as a scene from daily life, warlords terrorize the lower classes: "a peasant is stabbed by a soldier; above him, another peasant is restrained by his shirttail while a woman, hands in the air, cries out. At the lower right, a peasant is being stabbed in a chapel while his possessions are plundered, and nearby another peasant in fetters is cudgeled by a knight."[2] Violence pervaded every aspect of life: religion ("bloody crucifixes, threats of eternal damnation, and prurient depictions of mutilated saints"), travel ("brigands made travel a threat to life and limb, and ransoming captives was big business"), domestic living ("even the little people, too—the hatters, the tailors, the shepherds—were all quick to draw their knives"), and entertainment (throwing cats into bags, or beating pigs to death).[3] The government behaved no better than its subjects. Medieval Europeans suffered "centuries of institutionalized sadism," in which torture was practiced as a cruel art and "executions were orgies of sadism."[4]

Admittedly, for Pinker, this hyperviolent portrayal of the Middle Ages is a usable past. He is eager to tell his audience a shocking story. Dusting off Norbert Elias's hoary thesis, Pinker sees history as a story of progress, with occasional fits and starts and some moments of distinct regression, in which humanity engages slowly but resolutely in a civilizing process. Not only have we refined our manners and hygiene (a subject upon which Pinker deliberates with glee and graphic detail), but we have learned the necessity of restraint when it comes to emotion and physical response. At the heart of this evolution is the discovery of empathy. Beginning in the age of reason, Pinker explains, "people began to *sympathize* with more of their fellow humans, and were no longer indifferent to their sufferings."[5] In the twenty-first century, which Pinker describes as an age of empathy, our compassion extends even to the treatment of animals. As a result, according to Pinker, today we live in the most peaceful era in humanity's existence. For many, this story will seem implausible. After all, our capacity for destruction is unrivaled; in America we hear about mass shootings on almost a daily basis; and political scientists regularly speak of the modern era as the age of genocide. How can it be possible that humans were ever more bloodthirsty than we are today?

To make this startling, seemingly counterintuitive narrative a success, Pinker *needs* a barbaric Middle Ages. Indeed, without a violent point of departure, the book's central argument is untenable. Thus, it is not surprising that Pinker discovers a barbaric Middle Ages when he goes looking. However, as I hope to demonstrate, this preposterous caricature of the medieval world depends entirely on Pinker's ignorance of the sources that inform his statistics, coupled with a meager understanding of the medieval legal system.

The Sources

Pinker's brazen confidence in his hypothesis is helped greatly by the fact that he knows nothing about the medieval era. Indeed, the very suggestion that our medieval ancestors were morally underdeveloped betrays his ignorance of the fundamentals of the Middle Ages. Medieval Christians prized charity (*caritas*), best understood as neighborliness, as a key virtue. Men and women took seriously not only the church's Ten Commandments, but also the Seven Corporal Works of Mercy, ubiquitous in the era's artwork and the basis for its acclaimed hospitality.[6] One quickly discovers that Pinker's tacit refusal to read the work of actual historians is a boon to his cause. Only five medieval historians have made their way into his bibliography (Geary, Groebner, Hanawalt, Kaeuper, and Pérez), although their research plays a miniscule part in Pinker's historical analysis of the medieval era.[7]

To write a sensational history, you need sensational sources, and Pinker has had no difficulty finding sources about the Middle Ages that conform to his vision. His knowledge about violence in the medieval world is founded on four categories of source materials:

1. Grisly images of executions and torture devices, drawn from what Pinker refers to as "coffee table books" about the Inquisition, as well as the website of an Italian torture "museum" that purports to have a lofty but decidedly

ahistorical goal. The museum's website declares with pride that "the horror aroused in our visitors viewing the instruments allows us to make them our allies against torture"; in doing so, the exhibit "lays bare the worst side of human nature: every man hides and holds back a potential butcher."[8]

2. Arthurian romances, which Pinker treats as historical fact. Arthurian romances were intended to appeal to a knightly audience. A modern equivalent would be to regard the *Rambo* movies as an accurate depiction of the life of Vietnam veterans in America.

3. Bogus statistics. For the Middle Ages, Pinker draws on two highly unorthodox studies whose conspicuous titles publicize their spurious natures. In his *Great Big Book of Horrible Things,* and its accompanying website, "Death by Mass Unpleasantness," self-proclaimed "atrocitologist" Matthew White provides his reader with "necrometrics" (death tolls from across history) that are at the same time improbably specific and unbelievably high.[9] Political scientist Rudolf J. Rummel's *Death by Government* coins the term "democide" to describe the murderous activity of state systems. Each chapter heading takes its name from the death toll tied to a specific government (for example, "61,911,000 Murdered: The Soviet Gulag State"; "10,214,000 Murdered: The Depraved Nationalist Regime").[10] His numbers are also inflated: Rummel claims that 350,000 Jews were killed in the Spanish Inquisition, which is 1.7 times higher than the actual Jewish population of Spain at that time.[11]

4. Flawed historical crime statistics, compiled and analyzed by political scientist Ted R. Gurr and criminologist Manuel Eisner, both of whom rely on numbers furnished by medieval histories penned by James B. Given (thirteenth-century England) and Barbara A. Hanawalt (fourteenth-century England).[12] This is by far the most problematic of the four categories. While much of the other evidence, including White's and Rummel's statistics, can be easily dismissed as melodramatic nonsense, the same is not true of Gurr's and Eisner's works, which are academic in nature and which, on the surface, appear substantially more trustworthy. Nonetheless, the medieval data on which these studies are founded are inherently flawed: both Given and Hanawalt have been roundly criticized for their methodological approaches, and their statistics (although not their books) largely discredited.[13] I will elaborate on the disputes relating to their statistical usage below. More important still: Gurr and Eisner have little understanding of the context from which these numbers have been plucked; Pinker has none.

The Medieval Numbers

Statistics are the linchpin in Pinker's analysis. They are also the bread and butter of a psychologist's research. Pinker rails against advocacy groups who use "junk statistics" and make anecdote-driven claims; and yet, between his penchant for coffee table books and his failure to show any curiosity about the sources behind his statistics, Pinker has fallen into the exact same trap.[14] Without question, Pinker's objective is praiseworthy. Tracking rates of violence over time and space holds much promise for a better understanding of the dynamics of humanity's relationship with violence, and especially discerning those social and cultural factors that drive the human species to commit violent acts. Thus, it should come as no surprise that Pinker is not the first scholar to attempt such a comparison. However, as criticisms leveled at Given and Hanawalt make clear, it is an unachievable goal. No matter how great our desire to construct practical data from medieval European sources, we cannot make them conform to our needs.

Criminologists measure violence by the number of homicides per 100,000 population per year. In an era with reliable census data, as well as solid record keeping by the Bureau of Justice (or equivalent institutions in nations across the developed world), this approach produces reliable statistics that would seem to be an accurate reflection of modern rates of criminal violence. Yet, we need to acknowledge that the criminologist's tool was developed in response to modern data and a modern system of law. Medieval records present some insuperable obstacles, perhaps most significantly that we do not have accurate population figures for the period and estimates of population are problematic. Medieval England can serve as our example. The *Domesday Book* is as close as we can get to a medieval census, but its methodology is not conducive to population estimates. Its authors counted only heads of households, and thus dependents—women, children, singletons, and the elderly, all of whom comprise a larger segment of the population than householders—are omitted. So, too, are members of religious orders and the personnel who served and lived in castles. Major cities, like London or Winchester, also do not appear in the survey. Poll tax data for three years in the fourteenth century also exist, but they suffer from many of the same complications. Granted, none of this deterred Given from calculating estimates for his 1977 book, presumably the reason why both Gurr and Eisner have found his research so enthralling, although Given's enterprise produces figures that are "little more than guesswork," as mentioned by one critic.[15]

The deficit of population figures is just one impediment to producing crime rates for the medieval era. The corpus of medieval records is at best fragmentary, and it is not clear just what proportion of the records the extant rolls represent. For the county of Hampshire, for example, Carrie Smith explains that we have the reports of 12 coroners for the reigns of Edward III and Richard II, even though the Close Rolls (official collections of royal letters sent under seal) reveal that there were an additional 47 coroners elected during that 72-year period.[16] Coroners' enrollments were created with a distinct purpose: they acted as a check on the work of the jurors of the so-called Hundreds Courts (an administrative unit of a county), who were fined if they failed to report any criminal activity. Thus, once the rolls fulfilled their purpose, they were cancelled and, one suspects, disposed of accordingly.[17] It is not clear why some records survive, nor is it possible to determine if the extant rolls are typical, or whether we should assume that they survived because there was something exceptional about them.[18]

Granted, even if we had accurate population totals, and all records had survived, we would still find ourselves in trouble. Given and Hanawalt based their data on indictments rather than verdicts. The reason why they chose this approach is understandable. Nearly 72 percent of criminal perpetrators in medieval England fled; because there were no police forces, they were never tried.[19] Thus, trial verdicts represent an insignificant share of the crimes perpetrated. Calculating rates is further complicated by the fact that medieval juries were notoriously reluctant to convict. Conviction rates for homicide ranged between 12.5 and 21 percent (compared to a rate of 97.1 percent for American criminal cases in 2015).[20] Leery of the death penalty, medieval juries typically saw indictment itself as a worthy punishment for most offenders, because it meant time in prison awaiting trial, along with the discomfort and expense of a prison stay, as well as lost income and potentially irreparable damage to one's reputation within the community. Knowing this, it makes sense that Given and Hanawalt preferred indictments rather than convictions for comparative analysis. Yet, this puts us in the difficult situation of comparing apples and oranges.

We have high standards today for indictment: even if the state's prosecutors have met the legal requirements for the evidentiary bar, they might still fail to convince a grand jury of the defendant's guilt, preventing the case from going forward to trial. Medieval England's legal system had substantially different standards. Previous to the development of rules of evidence, rumor or suspicion alone was sufficient to secure an indictment. Given the ease of accusation, it is no surprise that malicious indictment (which would also throw off the reliability of a statistical comparison) was a serious problem.[21] The loose requirements for formal accusations, when combined with a somewhat rudimentary investigative process founded on paltry resources, surely suggest that some of those acquitted were in fact innocent of the charges. Indeed, given the high rate of flight, those few who stuck around to stand trial likely chose to do so because (a) they were innocent or (b) they were guilty, but not enough so to be condemned by a jury of their peers to death. Either way, if we rely on indictments rather than convictions in our statistical analysis, we end up in the uncomfortable situation experienced by Given and Hanawalt of "find[ing] the accused guilty *even if he has been acquitted.*"[22]

In addition, advances in modern medicine undoubtedly have had a weighty impact on rates of lethal violence. As Paul E. Hair remarked in his 1979 review of Given's book, in medieval England "corpses were often produced by incidents which nowadays would simply lead to visits to a doctor or short spells in hospital."[23] To name just a few wonders of the modern medical world that we take for granted: knowledge of germ theory and the value of surgical hygiene; blood transfusions; surgery with anesthetics; x-ray and ultrasound technologies; antibiotics; pain relief. Most people who are shot or stabbed today survive; the same was not true in the Middle Ages. Without anesthetics, surgery intended to heal sent some patients into shock. Without antibiotics, festering wounds turned fatal. Even more problematic, medical theory of the time understood infection as a key stage in the healing process. If a wound did not infect naturally, English surgeons were advised to contaminate it in order to speed the process along.[24] And what about infanticide? The medieval world knew nothing about SIDS, which today claims as many as 92.6 deaths per 100,000 live births per year.[25] Philip Gavitt contends that deaths by SIDS in the late medieval era were routinely mistaken for smothering deaths blamed on wet nurses.[26] Clearly, the differences in medical knowledge and technology alone makes a statistical comparison between the two eras impracticable.

The greatest hurdle in assessing rates of crime for medieval England is the simple fact that we cannot take medieval indictments at face value. Private accusers frequently employed legal fiction as a strategy to work around the limitations of a rigid common law. To offer two typical examples: (1) In general, litigants preferred the impartial justice and speedy resolution of the king's court to local judgment. Thus, they subtly enhanced the nature of their accusations in order to have their cases adjudicated by the king's justices. Asserting that it was a breach of the king's peace (*contra pacem*), that an assault transpired with force and arms (*vi et armis*), or that a theft exceeded 40 shillings were recognized legal fictions exercised to bring one's case into the king's jurisdiction.[27] (2) Use of the "bill of Middlesex" is perhaps the most widely acknowledged legal fiction. In order to have one's case of debt brought before the King's Bench (a substantially more efficient option than the Court of Common Pleas), the accuser fabricated a suit for criminal trespass within Westminster, where the King's Bench had criminal jurisdiction as the local court. Once the defendant was in prison, the fictitious suit was dropped altogether, and the accuser moved forward with a suit of debt before the King's Bench.[28] In both of these situations, the criminal allegations were baseless.

Private accusers were not alone in manipulating the law. When juries believed the circumstances of a homicide did not warrant the death penalty, they were content to adapt the details of the record to secure a pardon. Thus, under the supportive guidance of the indicting jury, the man who discovered his wife in flagrante with another man and then swiftly hacked the lover to death was transformed into a victim backed into a corner, lashing out only when he had no alternative because his life was in imminent danger.[29] Alteration of the facts of the case did not happen in all or even most indictments. Yet, without a side-by-side comparison of the case details across the legal record (from inquest to indictment to trial)—an accomplishment that is rarely possible because of the poor survival rate of records—there is no way to discern whether jurors tampered with the facts of the case. Legal fiction also pervades accusations of rape leveled against medieval England's clergy. Disgruntled with the inability of their parish clergy to live out their vows of celibacy, angry parishioners took the law into their own hands by accusing them of rape. In doing so, they knew full well that their unruly priests would not be executed as criminals. Benefit of clergy removed priests from the king's courts to the bishop's, where at long last a clergyman would have to answer with penance for his (albeit consensual) sexual transgressions, which was in fact the purpose of indicting him in the first place.[30]

To make the situation even more complicated, crimes then did not necessarily mean the same thing as they do today. Take the crime of rape, for example. The Latin verb used to describe the crime of "rape" is *rapio, rapere,* which means "to seize." Building on this broader sense of the term, the legal indictments employ it chiefly in two scenarios: (1) coitus without consent, and (2) ravishment, that is, nonconsensual abduction. In both cases, the consent at issue was not necessarily the victim's, but her husband's or her father's. The former category sometimes also included headstrong women who chose to marry against their fathers' will.[31] In the latter situation, most women had not only consented to their abductions, but they had their bags packed and were ready to go.[32] Indeed, all too often a woman's "rapist" was a family member helping her to leave an abusive marriage.[33] Close attention to the indictment's language can help us to discern which "rapes" also comprised sexual assault. Presenting juries included "lexical doublets," a phrase coined by Caroline Dunn, such as *rapuit et cognovit carnaliter* ("he raped her and carnally knew her") versus *rapuit et abduxit* ("he raped and abducted her") to clarify the nature of the offense.[34] However, all of the other problems above are still associated with the existing records.

Other offenses that we today would categorize as criminal belonged in the medieval world to a more loosely defined civil jurisdiction and thus were not recorded among the crown pleas. Drawing blood, affray, assault, wounding, riot, and mayhem might be sued in a wide variety of courts, and thus appear scattered among the civil jurisdictions of local, royal, and ecclesiastical courts. Criminal jurisdiction also failed to include those crimes perpetrated against or involving the clergy. Thus, any study concentrating exclusively on criminal records cannot offer a complete picture of medieval violence.

Pinker has never seen a medieval court record, nor does he understand how the law worked in the Middle Ages. Therefore, it is no surprise that none of the above is factored into his discussion of the medieval numbers. When he measures medieval against modern statistics, he has no idea that they are measuring very different things; without valid statistics, Pinker's entire argument falls apart. He cannot maintain that violence has declined since the Middle Ages because we have no real evidence to prove that it has. Indeed, it is not at all clear just how violent the Middle Ages actually were.

The Historiographic Context

In Pinker's mind, convincing his audience of the brutality of the Middle Ages is somehow a herculean endeavor; yet, for medievalists, the more usual complaint is the seemingly natural conflation between "medieval" and "barbaric." In large part, this is because Elias, while new to Pinker, is certainly not new to historians.[35] Elias's theory of the civilizing process is the foundation for studies of historical violence and has been reenergized through new conceptualizations multiple times since its publication in 1939. Without a doubt, the most thought provoking has been Michel Foucault's *Discipline and Punish: The Birth of the Prison* (1975). Foucault raised the stakes considerably, seeing medieval monarchies wielding terror as a tool of state building. In order to compel resistance to the ever-increasing reach of centralized government, the state sponsored public spectacles of violence, stamping punishment on the bodies of those who failed to show adequate respect when faced with authority.[36] While Foucault's work does not appear in Pinker's bibliography, his shadow hangs heavily over the study, with its focus on democide.

Grappling with Foucault's equally sensationalist and ahistorical views over the past 42 years has prompted medievalists to question just how accurate his perception of the medieval era actually is. No one disagrees with the view that the medieval world was violent: it was. Medieval sermon stories regularly depict an angry God taking out his vengeance upon man by spreading disease, brewing up storms, setting fire to homes and villages, and causing sudden death. Focus on the crucifixion and the suffering of Christ encouraged self-violence, from starvation to flagellation and more, as the life of Henry Suso, a doctor of the church who slept on a bed of nails and wore a life-sized cross fastened to his back for a period of eight years, implies.[37] The church did not waver in assigning flogging or prison terms to a penitent when the nature of the sin required it. Medieval law prescribed public hanging, burning, blinding, and castration for felonies, and clergymen heartily recommended all devout Christians attend as a deterrent from choosing a criminal lifestyle. If violence is a learned trait, medieval men certainly learned it at home, as husbands were expected to govern their wives, children, and servants with a firm hand.[38] Yet, all of this is still a far cry from the budding panopticism outlined by Foucault.

The historical community's response to Foucault's thesis might have warned Pinker off from writing his book, had he made the effort to read any of it. Foucault's history is a paradigm of the danger inherent in arguing from theory rather than evidence. In reality, violence in the Middle Ages was hardly a "spectacle." The English sent only the most hardened criminals to their deaths. "Hangman" was not even a profession in medieval England, as there was not enough work to keep a man employed.[39] Indeed, far from the "orgies of sadism" that Pinker envisions, medieval executions were "commonly hole-in-corner affairs, with few witnesses," and rather than delighting in the pain of the executed, those present participated in a heart-rending salvific drama intended to reconcile the penitent with the Christian community before death.[40] Treason trials were the one exception to the rule. They were intended to be gruesome. When Dafydd ap Gruffydd was executed, he was drawn to the site of execution, hanged, his entrails burned while he was still alive, beheaded, and then quartered, his body parts dispersed throughout England to be displayed as a warning to other potential rebels.[41] However, only a handful of political traitors received this kind of treatment over the course of the Middle Ages, again falling short of Pinker's imaginative bar.

Even the use of torture in the medieval period was tamer than either Foucault or Pinker present. It is important to note that the English did not employ torture, but during the thirteenth century, Continental courts revived the Roman practice, exclusively for the purpose of extracting a confession, not as a punishment itself, as Pinker writes.[42] Torture was not part of the normal legal process; rather, it was a last resort, for those instances in which the defendant was presumed guilty, but the evidence did not meet the *ius commune*'s high evidentiary standards of two eyewitnesses or a confession. Furthermore, the law set restrictions on its implementation: torture was to be used only in capital crimes; the defendant was not to be maimed or killed; a physician had to be present at all times; torture might not be applied for longer than it takes to say a prayer; and so on.[43] When it came to the legal treatment of heretics or witches, a loosening of the rules inevitably transpired, but the inquisitor was not given carte blanche to do as he pleased.

The king's officials were even less competent when it comes to punishing the bodies of offenders. As far back as the twelfth-century *Leis Willelme*, English law prescribed castration and blinding for rape, treason, poaching, and a miscellany of other crimes. Physical mutilation was intended as a merciful alternative to capital punishment. Yet, finding instances outside of literature in which these penalties were actually carried out has not been as easy as one might think. More typically, the violence enacted by the state targeted one's purse.[44] For readers of Foucault and Pinker, fines and compensation are a much less "sexy" means of punishing offenders, but it was an effective means of law enforcement.

Conclusion

What rankles medievalists most about Steven Pinker's book is that he is not particularly interested in the Middle Ages. Rather, the era is simply a starting point from which to apply a well-worn historical theory while adding his own psychological twist. However, in doing so, Steven Pinker dabbles in history, without bothering to acknowledge that it is a discipline with its own rules and methods. One can imagine that Pinker might empathize with the historian's outrage if an amateur psychologist without even a rudimentary exposure to psychological theory tried to rebuild the pedestal from which Sigmund Freud had fallen years ago. Nevertheless, in this respect, historians need to acknowledge that Pinker is not the problem; he is merely a symptom. Among even educated people today, history is not often understood as a concrete discipline requiring training and experience, like physics or mathematics. Historians have not worked hard enough to convey to the world what we do: in particular, we do not just read the work of other historians and regurgitate it from a slightly different angle. In my case, being a historian means spending days and weeks in distant, sometimes inaccessible, archives, reading grimy, handwritten, and abbreviated documents in Latin or Anglo-Norman Law French; reading reams upon reams of historians' work to make sure that I understand how my perspective fits in with theirs (or not); and being able to perform the historical analysis that makes sense of everything I read in the archives.

Despite the dubious nature of Pinker's history, the response to his book has an important lesson for historians: Pinker's message is reaching the masses, and ours is not. Why aren't academic histories read as voraciously as their popular counterparts? Surely, *that* is the question we need to address next.

Sara M. Butler is King George III Professor in British History at The Ohio State University. She has written on the subjects of marital violence, suicide, abortion, and divorce in medieval England. Her most recent book is Forensic Medicine and Death Investigation in Medieval England *(London: Routledge, 2015).*

Notes

1. Steven Pinker, *The Better Angels of Our Nature: Why Violence Has Declined* (New York: Penguin Books, 2011), 1, 132.
2. Pinker, *Better Angels,* 65–66.
3. Ibid., 67–68.
4. Ibid., 130, 132.
5. Ibid., 133.
6. The Seven Corporal Works of Mercy are based on the teachings of Christ, and include: (1) to feed the hungry, (2) to give water to the thirsty, (3) to clothe the naked, (4) to shelter the homeless, (5) to visit the sick, (6) to visit the imprisoned, or ransom the captive, and (7) to bury the dead.
7. Patrick Geary, *The Myth of Nations: The Medieval Origins of Europe* (Princeton, NJ: Princeton University Press, 2002); Valentin Groebner, "Losing Face, Saving Face: Noses and Honour in the Late Medieval Town," *History Workshop Journal* 40 (1995): 1–15; Barbara A. Hanawalt, "Violent Death in Fourteenth- and early Fifteenth-Century England," *Contemporary Studies in Society & History* 18, no. 3 (1976): 297–320; Richard W. Kaeuper, "Chivalry and the 'Civilizing Process,'" in *Violence in Medieval Society,* ed. Richard W. Kaeuper (Rochester, NY: Boydell & Brewer, 2000), 22–38; Joseph Pérez, *The Spanish Inquisition: A History* (New Haven, CT: Yale University Press, 2006).
8. For example, Robert Held, *Inquisition: A Selected Survey of the Collection of Torture Instruments from the Middle Ages to Our Times* (Aslockton: Avon & Arno, 1986); and

Museo della Tortura e della Pena di Morte (San Gimignano, Italy), http://www .torturemuseum.it/en/ (accessed 12 October 2017).

9. Matthew White, *The Great Big Book of Horrible Things: The Definitive Chronicle of History's 100 Worst Atrocities* (New York: Norton, 2011). Since the writing of Pinker's book, White's website has migrated to: Matthew White, "Necrometrics" (2010–2014), http://necrometrics.com/ (accessed 12 October 2017).

10. Rudoph J. Rummel, *Death by Government* (New Brunswick, NJ: Transaction Publishers, 1994).

11. Pinker, *Better Angels*, 141; Helen Rawlings, *The Spanish Inquisition* (Malden, MA: Blackwell, 2006), 48.

12. James B. Given, *Society and Homicide in Thirteenth-Century England* (Stanford, CA: Stanford University Press, 1977); and Barbara A. Hanawalt, *Crime and Conflict in English Communities, 1300–1348* (Cambridge, MA: Harvard University Press, 1979).

13. In his review of Given's book, Roy F. Hunnisett observed that his statistics "are riddled with inaccuracies." R. F. Hunnisett, review of *Society and Homicide in Thirteenth-Century England, History* 63, no. 209 (1978): 445.

14. Pinker, *Better Angels*, 401, 403.

15. Edward Powell, "Social Research and the Use of Medieval Criminal Records," *Michigan Law Review* 79, no. 4 (1981): 975.

16. Carrie Smith, "Medieval Coroners' Rolls: Legal Fiction or Historical Fact?," in *Courts, Counties and the Capital in the Later Middle Ages,* ed. Diana E. S. Dunn (New York: St. Martin's Press, 1996), 97–98.

17. David Crook, *Records of the General Eyre,* Public Record Office Handbooks, no. 20 (London: PRO, 1982), 36.

18. For a more detailed discussion of medieval coroners' rolls, see R. F. Hunnisett, *The Medieval Coroner* (Cambridge: Cambridge University Press, 1961), chap. 6.

19. Bernard William McLane, "Juror Attitudes toward Local Disorder: The Evidence of the 1328 Trailbaston Proceedings," in *Twelve Good Men and True*, ed. James S. Cockburn and Thomas A. Green (Princeton, NJ: Princeton University Press, 1988), 36–64, here 56.

20. John G. Bellamy, *The Criminal Trial in Later Medieval England* (Toronto: University of Toronto Press, 1998), 69; Patti B. Saris et al., "Overview of Federal Criminal Cases Fiscal Year 2015" (Washington, DC: United States Sentencing Commission, June 2016), 4, http://www.ussc.gov/sites/default/files/pdf/research-and-publi cations/research-publications/2016/FY15_Overview_Federal_Criminal_Cases .pdf (accessed 13 October 2017).

21. Jonathan Rose, *Maintenance in Medieval England* (Cambridge: Cambridge University Press, 2017), 80.

22. Powell, "Social Research," 969; emphasis in original.

23. Paul E. Hair, review of *Society and Homicide in Thirteenth-Century England, Population Studies* 33, no. 1 (1979): 196–197, here 196.

24. R. Theodore Beck, *The Cutting Edge: Early History of the Surgeons of London* (London: Lund Humphries, 1974), 12. Whether to infect the wound was a subject of some controversy. See Carole Rawcliffe, *Medicine and Society in Later Medieval England* (London: Sandpiper Books, 1995), 74.

25. Center for Disease Control and Prevention, "Sudden Unexpected Infant Death and Sudden Infant Death Syndrome," US Department of Health and Human Services, https://www.cdc.gov/sids/data.htm (accessed 13 October 2017).

26. Philip Gavitt, "Infant Death in Late Medieval Florence: The Smothering Hypothesis Reconsidered," in *Medieval Family Roles: A Book of Essays,* ed. Cathy Jorgensen Itnyre (New York: Garland, 1996), 137–157.

27. S. F. C. Milsom, "Trespass from Henry III to Edward III," *Law Quarterly Review* 74 (1958): 195–224, here 222–223; Michael Lobban, "Legal Fictions before the Age of Reform," in *Legal Fictions in Theory and Practice,* ed. Maksymilian Del Mar and William Twining (Heidelberg: Springer, 2015), 200.

28. S. F. C. Milsom, *Historical Foundations of the Common Law* (London: Butterworths, 1969), 54–59.

29. Thomas A. Green, *Verdict According to Conscience: Perspectives on the English Criminal Trial Jury, 1200–1800* (Chicago: University of Chicago Press, 1985), 42–43.

30. Robin L. Storey, "Malicious Indictments of Clergy in the Fifteenth Century," in *Medieval Ecclesiastical Studies: In Honour of Dorothy M. Owen,* ed. M. J. Franklin and Christopher Harper-Bill (Woodbridge: Boydell, 1995), 221–240.

31. James A. Brundage, "Rape and Marriage in the Medieval Canon Law," in *Sex, Law and Marriage in the Middle Ages,* ed. James A. Brundage (Aldershot, UK: Variorum, 1993), 62–75, here 74.

32. Sue Sheridan Walker, "Punishing Convicted Ravishers: Statutory Strictures and Actual Practice in Thirteenth- and Fourteenth-Century England," *Journal of Medieval History* 13, no. 3 (1987): 237–249, here 238.

33. Sara M. Butler, *Divorce in Medieval England: From One to Two Persons in Law* (New York: Routledge, 2013), 66–71.

34. Caroline Dunn, *Stolen Women in Medieval England* (Cambridge: Cambridge University Press, 2013), 33.

35. Pinker describes Norbert Elias as "the most important thinker you have never heard of." Pinker, *Better Angels,* 59.

36. Michel Foucault, *Discipline and Punish: The Birth of the Prison,* trans. Alan Sheridan (New York: Pantheon Books, 1977).

37. For more on Henry Suso, see chapter 12 of Jerome Kroll and Bernard Bachrach, *The Mystic Mind: The Psychology of Medieval Mystics and Ascetics* (New York: Routledge, 2005).

38. Sara M. Butler, *The Language of Abuse: Marital Violence in Later Medieval England* (Leiden: Brill, 2007).

39. Henry Summerson, "Attitudes to Capital Punishment in England, 1220–1350," in *Thirteenth Century England VIII: Proceedings of the Durham Conference 1999,* ed. Michael Prestwich, Richard Britnell, and Robin Frame (Woodbridge, UK: Boydell, 2001), 123–133, here 128.

40. Summerson, "Attitudes to Capital Punishment," 130; Trisha Olson, "The Medieval Blood Sanction and the Divine Beneficience of Pain: 1100–1450," *Journal of Law and Religion* 22, no. 1 (2006): 63–129.

41. Katherine Royer, "The Body in Parts: Reading the Execution Ritual in Late Medieval England," *Historical Reflections* 29, no. 2 (2003): 319–339, here 328–329.

42. Pinker, *Better Angels,* 146.

43. Edward Peters, *Torture* (Philadelphia: University of Pennsylvania Press, 1985), chap. 2.

44. Daniel Lord Smail, "Violence and Predation in Late Medieval Mediterranean Europe," *Comparative Studies in Society and History* 54, no. 1 (2012): 7–34.

Chapter 4

The Complexity of History
Russia and Steven Pinker's Thesis

Nancy Shields Kollmann

It feels churlish to disagree with Steven Pinker's feel-good argument that face-to-face violence has declined in world history over the last six or so centuries. He does indeed show with statistical and anecdotal evidence that in many places the modern world is less hazardous to one's personal survival than life in premodern times, and that attitudes in many societies have changed. But historians can be a churlish bunch, and reading his book leaves me wanting more specificity and more difference, and leery of so long, broad, and universalizing an argument. I find the most intriguing part of the book, in fact, to be the exceptions Pinker cites to his observed patterns. When I consider early modern Russia, what strikes me are the ways in which Russia took a very different approach to violence, even though some of the same influences were at play.

Pinker writes on a vast scale: he argues that rates of face-to-face violence and organized warfare have fallen and attitudes have turned against violence in "civilized" societies, expanding from Europe into contemporary global society. As roots of these changes he identifies phenomena familiar to historians thanks to burgeoning literature since the 1970s: early modern European state building, "the civilizing process," and the decline in homicide rates.[1]

Central to Pinker's argument is the rise of a centralized state ("Leviathan") that claimed a monopoly of violence and enforced it through policing and judicial punishment. Important here is that the state was well run, preferably in a way that moved toward democracy and pluralism over time; buying into the political system encouraged citizens to maintain peace. A second key element is the expansion of interregional commerce, which gave communities and individuals incentives to cooperate for individual and mutual benefit. "Gentle commerce" also had the benefit of encouraging the growth of cities, which Pinker finds statistically less violent than rural communities. Third is the spread of so-called civilized behavior, initially inculcated through etiquette designed to corral violence among the king's men and create a "courtly" culture of disciplined servants to the crown. Later this trend was reinforced with Enlightenment claims for the universality of human rights, which in turn spawned a revulsion toward bodily harm to living creatures (animal and human) and eventually empathy for minority rights. As for the engines of these changes, Pinker relies on psychology, both group and individual, to argue that people, groups, and states assess violence by cost-benefit analysis. They calculate the risks to their self-interest, honor, and basic survival of engaging in, or deferring, violence. Thus, he also extols the rise of reason as a foundation on which individuals can make such calculations. From the sixteenth century, he argues, these forces joined together to launch a more "civilized" world, where educated people living in urbanized democracies with healthy economies grew to avoid violence; Pinker marshals ample statistical evidence of homicide rates, loss in war, and frequency of armed combat, as well as anecdotal evidence of growing revulsion toward violence. In the very big picture, life in the stereotypical European civilized society has indeed improved.

Pinker also acknowledges exceptions. He notes that the dominant ideology of the nineteenth century—ethnic nationalism—undermines claims for universal rights, and he identifies geographical areas that did not experience a decline of violence. In addition to isolated, often mountainous regions, he identifies a baleful arc of contemporary countries stretching from Central and East Africa through northern India to Southeast Asia beset by a more violent status quo.[2] Poverty, weak and corrupt states, and the absence of literacy and effective civic education deflect these areas from a more peaceable path. Most importantly, he argues that a decline in violence is "not inevitable": these trends have always stemmed from rational choice and are not dependent on supposed inner demons of human nature. Societies and individuals could choose more war, more discrimination, more ethnic cleansing, and more ambient violence if they find it in their self-interest. It is up to us.

In broad sweeps Pinker's argument does jibe with what many of us experience today. The historian in me, however, worries. His Eurocentrism raises a flag: he implies a single path into a peaceable modernity following the European model, leaving one to wonder about paths not taken, or the very concept of a determined path. Additionally, his focus on rational agency implies that other states or societies might have combined his cited factors and others to different ends. This seems to be the case for early modern Russia.

I have analyzed the practice of criminal law in early modern Russia from the sixteenth through the eighteenth centuries with the problem of violence as a main concern.[3] Violence was on my mind for two reasons: since the sixteenth century (and reiterated in Cold War rhetoric) Europeans have characterized Russians and their society as despotic, brutal, and less civilized than the European "West."[4] Second, I had in mind the Foucauldian paradigm, supported by research by Spierenburg, Linebaugh, van Dülmen, and others, that held that some European states well into the seventeenth century ruled through terror by staging "spectacles of execution," compensating for the inability to rule through law, policing, and civic cooperation with displays of official brutality. Eventually European states were able to abandon theatrical public executions, cruel and unusual punishments, judicial torture, and other public displays of violence because of two interconnected trends: a growing state capacity to police deviant behavior and to inculcate civic values in its citizens, and a growing public acceptance of humanitarian ideals.[5]

Violence was not the only issue I was concerned with; I also analyzed the degree to which the tsar's criminal courts ruled in accordance with law and legal procedure. I read the law and case law of homicide, recidivist theft and robbery, and major political and religious crime (in Muscovy's theocratic ideology, witchcraft, heresy, treason, and rebellion all qualified as assaults on the state). Trial transcripts ranged from the early seventeenth century well into the eighteenth and covered the empire, involving not only the dominant East Slavic population but also subject peoples in Siberia, the Middle Volga (Tatar and Finno-Ugric peoples), Ukraine, and even European foreigners in Russian service.

I found that the early modern Russian judicial system was in some ways less violent than its European counterparts. I cannot make this argument on the basis of statistics. Rates of crime are unavailable: no statistical data was kept (police forces were not functioning efficiently across the empire until late in the nineteenth century). Certain types of crime garnered especial attention over time, possibly suggesting new outbreaks. Predictably, Russia's earliest criminal law codes acknowledge prosecutions and punishment up to execution for murder, arson, and other major crimes as well as for political and religious crimes. As the state began to amass bureaucratic control in the sixteenth century, recidivist burglary and theft, often identified with professional banditry in the countryside, became a special concern. Legal procedure and criminal police institutions were created and endured through the seventeenth century. A massive legal compilation in 1649 for the first time gave detailed legal treatment to political and religious crimes against the state, reflecting Muscovy's expanding control over peasant labor, taxation, and daily life. In response, the seventeenth century saw a rising incidence of peasants fleeing landlords; when Peter I (r. 1682–1725) instituted an onerous poll tax on peasants as well as new military recruitment for a massively increased standing army and new navy, runaway soldiers and sailors joined the ranks of runaway serfs as a focus of criminal prosecution. Persecutions of religious heterodoxy proliferated from the late seventeenth century after a theological schism in the Orthodox Church; for more than a century thereafter, official persecution of "Old Believer" communities waxed and waned. The most recalcitrant of these schismatics were imprisoned and executed by burning as heretics. While we cannot attach rates of incidence to these crimes, it is clear that as the early modern Russian state expanded, it encountered violent challenges to its claims to control labor, collect taxes, maintain public order, and enforce ideology.

Other early modern European states faced similar challenges, but Russia's modes of governance and criminal justice seem to have relied less on overt violence to meet them. We can see this in many spheres. One is the state's ability to monopolize the means of violence: in the fifteenth and sixteenth centuries Moscow's rulers systematically integrated previously sovereign princes and local elites and their private retinues into the grand prince's army. Deprived of sovereign rights, such princes and elites in return received social status, land grants, and other largesse. Well compensated in an environment with few other opportunities for gain, Russia's elite made its peace with service to the tsar and was remarkably stable well into the eighteenth century, with astoundingly few episodes of opposition to the dynasty.

In addition to monopolizing the means of violence in this way, Moscow's grand princes (self-titled tsars after 1547) assiduously condemned private violence among individuals, clans, and other social groups; dueling and vendettas were forbidden and harshly punished. In their place, the state offered redress through litigation over insult to honor. All subjects of the tsar, from the highest church hierarchs and secular elites to serfs and even slaves, could litigate against people of all social ranks, and they did. Offenses were usually verbal, occasionally including affronts such as knocking off a woman's hat or pulling a man's beard; such insults often occurred together with physical assault, but the crimes were tried separately. As a rule, winning litigants were compensated with a fine, whose size rose according to the social rank of the insulted, and with the satisfaction of a restored reputation. When Europeans imported dueling in the late seventeenth century, the state immediately clamped down, punishing it as a capital crime. Peter I even ordered not only that a victorious dueler be executed by hanging, but that the corpse of his rival also be strung up.[6]

In Russia the reach of the criminal law was intentionally narrow: it involved murder and recidivist theft and robbery, arson and other heinous crimes, and high political and religious crime. Petty crimes that in some contemporary European countries were punished up to capital punishment were in Russia left to communities to deal with. Similarly, the reach of the central government was intentionally limited: it focused on monopolizing violence, collecting resources, and dispensing the criminal law. Otherwise, as a multiethnic Eurasian "empire of difference," the central government allowed subject peoples to retain language, religion, court systems, elites, and public services as before; similarly, the East Slavic peasant majority lived under the authority of landlords or village communes. All these communities were entitled to use corporal punishment for petty crime and disorder, according to local tradition. But none was allowed to impinge on the criminal process; if a murder, robbery, witchcraft accusation, or other major crime occurred in a village, noble estate, or native tribe, leaders were required to turn in suspects to the local governor for state justice. Those who tried to solve serious cases on their own, or administered torture, were punished harshly. Having defined the criminal law narrowly, the state worked assiduously to control that arena.[7]

The state also struggled, as all empires did, with policing officialdom to avoid corruption, violence, and abuse. Truly egregious cases of corrupt governors, often in far-flung Siberia where the riches of the furs and the China trade tempted graft, were prosecuted harshly; as a preventative measure, the state rotated governors every two years, never sold venalities, and never let local notables develop regional power. Since the state understood that in Siberia and steppe borderlands subject peoples could disappear into the forest or prairie if the state demanded too much, governors were explicitly ordered not to abuse the locals. Such prescriptions hardly prevented violence against natives: initial stages of conquest were bloody and Russian garrisons ensured the constant threat of violence. But these approaches to local governance reflect the state's aversion to violence when it contradicted its goals.[8]

For similar reasons the early modern Russian state sharply contrasts to many European counterparts in its approach to Christianization; the state refused to allow the Orthodox Church to forcibly convert non-Orthodox subjects, again for the pragmatic goal of not alienating the tax-paying populace. The Orthodox Church was not in any case a strongly missionary faith: it never developed a rhetoric of religiously sanctioned violence akin to crusades and its moral philosophy advocated personal restraint, inner reformation, and mercy. Exceptions were two periods of forcible conversion of Muslims in the Middle Volga and Bashkiria in the eighteenth century; these were fueled to some extent by religious zeal connected to Catholic influence at court, but primarily by Russian migration into these valuable farming territories. Conversion served as a weapon with which to appropriate lands from uncooperative Muslims. But, as a rule, the state restrained forcible conversion precisely to maintain stable governance and taxation across the empire.[9]

Since Russia was an autocracy with no representative institutions or enfranchised social classes to provide leverage against the state, its legal system might be expected to have been arbitrary and despotic. Foreign visitors certainly alleged as much. My study shows, however, that the criminal law was applied in a systematic manner according to the law. Law codes that included criminal punishments and procedure were issued in 1497, 1550, 1649, and 1669, supplemented by myriad decrees from chanceries with judicial authority. These laws and decrees were laconic and practical, rarely theoretical or generalizable, but they provided judges with bases for trials and judgments. Judges themselves, however, were untrained in the law. Military officers, they were appointed to be jacks-of-all-trades with adjudication a low priority among more pressing military, fiscal, and administrative roles. Legal expertise, therefore, resided with the scribes assigned to their offices. Trained in the law according to uniform standards of procedure and paperwork emanating from Moscow, the local scribe kept judges on track with instructions on procedure and citations from the law regarding sentencing. Across the empire, transcripts of court cases follow the same model, use the same language, quote the same laws, and reach the appropriate verdict—an amazing uniformity across a huge empire when compared to the legal multiplicity that many European countries faced at the time. The law distinguished levels of violence in punishment, reserving capital punishment for the highest crimes. To cite one example, a Tunguz tribe in eastern Siberia demanded that the judge turn over a Russian accused of killing one of their princes for execution by tribal justice. The governor insisted that the tsar's law prevailed; finding the man guilty of unintentional homicide, not murder, they sentenced him to a "merciless" flogging, much to the dissatisfaction of the Tunguz.[10]

Other aspects of criminal practice also mitigated the use of violence. One was the provision of mercy: judges often reduced sentences in the tsar's name to respond to community appeals or otherwise maintain social stability.[11] In Russia mercy reinforced the patrimonial tenet of Muscovite political ideology that the tsar was a just judge who protected his people from harm. Secondly, from the late seventeenth century, laws reduced the incidence of the death penalty, sending many capital criminals to exile to Siberia or other frontier towns. Exile was not an imprisonment system; the convict was kept in place by sheer distance and by branding for the most serious of them. While in exile, criminals worked: peasants farmed, artisans practiced their crafts, many joined the local governor's militia. Reducing capital punishment in favor of exile addressed Russia's chronic shortage of labor.[12]

Even more unlike its European peers, Russia did not practice the elaborate, theatrical "spectacles of suffering" for public executions that have garnered such attention in early modern European criminal law. In Russia, executions were simple affairs; the judge was expected to gather a crowd, often on a market day, as soon as possible after the verdict. He was to have the verdict read aloud and then to execute promptly, generally by hanging or beheading. The 1649 law code prescribed that the condemned be given six weeks to repent, but case law shows that this was rarely observed. Neither did courts take the time to assemble multiple condemned criminals for mass execution, or to build viewing bleachers and impressive scaffolds. They did not have formal rituals of last meals, forgiveness of the executioner, additional tortures on the stand, and gruesome executions such as quartering. Rather, the terror of executions in Muscovy might have been in their speed; with Moscow so far away and cases dragging on for months and more with consultation between center and local courts, communities needed to be reminded that the tsar's law really meant business. Judges were told "not to delay the tsar's work" (perhaps also a hedge against their being bribed) and they took pains to report back to Moscow how promptly they had indeed carried out an execution.

Russia's pragmatic approach to violence in the criminal process changed somewhat with exposure to European practice. Before the 1690s, a few incidences of the horrific punishment of quartering are cited, but they were exceptional.[13] Peter I came to power formally in 1682 as a ten-year-old and famously surrounded himself with European officers as he was growing up; not surprisingly, European-style tortures and executions begin to appear in his day. In 1696 a deserter was sentenced to breaking on the wheel, the first mention of such punishment in Russia; in 1697 Peter I staged a beheading in a theatrical manner, with the blood of the executed flowing over the exhumed body of a political accomplice of the convicted. But it was firsthand experience in Europe that brought the full "spectacle of execution" model to Russia. Peter I witnessed a mass execution in Amsterdam during his embassy abroad (1697–1698) and staged a similar spectacle in Moscow in 1698 when he dashed back to Russia to suppress a musketeer rebellion. Upward to one thousand people were tortured and over seven hundred were executed in mass groups in several "days" of execution, while others were flogged, exiled, or otherwise punished (Illustration 4.1). Breaking on the wheel and beheading with a sword (not the customary Russian axe) were European innovations here, as well as the vast scale of the spectacle itself. Hundreds were hanged from the Kremlin walls, their bodies left to sit all winter; hundreds more were beheaded; priests were broken on the wheel.[14]

During his reign Peter I resorted to such spectacles in a few exceptional cases of high treason and official corruption, but in rural settings, executions continued to be simple, speedy affairs. Conversely, however, Peter I further limited the use of the death penalty by requiring that each capital sentence be reviewed and by expanding the capital crimes to be punished with exile in Siberia or to forced labor on his many new construction projects, such as canals, harbors, and St. Petersburg. At the dawn of the eighteenth century, Russia's use of the death penalty was declining.

Unlike any European counterpart, in the 1740s Russia abolished the death penalty entirely, replacing it with exile upon order of Peter I's daughter, Empress Elizabeth I (r. 1741–1761). There followed a great expansion of the exile and forced labor systems and a greater elaboration of brandings and bodily mutilation to mark capital criminals in exile. Although motives of the abolition were never overtly explained, and the abolition was not codified clearly, executions for common crime ended. Empress Elizabeth's motivation might have been religious, or she might have been reacting to the

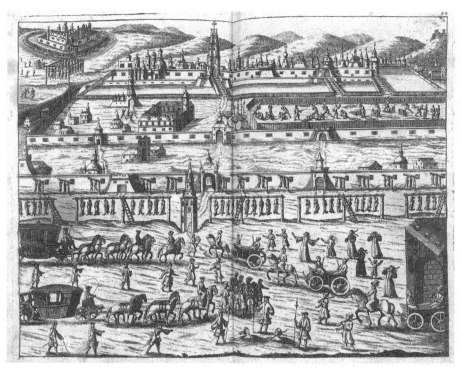

Illustration 4.1   Russia's first "spectacle of execution": "The Execution of Musketeers, Moscow 1698," published in Johann-Georg Korb, *Diarium itineris in Moscoviam* (Vienna, 1700). With permission of the Library of the Hoover Institution, Stanford, CA.

conditions of her coming to the throne. In the late 1730s the ruling faction under Empress Anna Ioannovna (r. 1730–1740) had executed political rivals in a display of unprecedented violence that shocked the nobility. Another faction then brought Elizabeth to power in a coup. Her abolition of the death penalty might have been intended to assuage noble fears. The nobility's continued Europeanization and the spread of Enlightenment humanitarian values under Catherine II (r. 1762–1796) ensured the continuation of the policy. Catherine, inspired by Beccaria, also lobbied for the abolition of torture, which occurred in 1801. Alexander I (r. 1801–1825) spoke proudly of imposing Russia's more benevolent law on newly acquired territories such as Georgia, where capital punishment was still being practiced. In the first half of the nineteenth century, brutality in the law was gradually lessened, with privileged social ranks receiving immunity from corporal punishment, the abolition of the branding of female exiles, and, eventually, the ending of bodily mutilation and flogging entirely, and other mitigations.[15]

This is not to say that executions disappeared entirely; although this was not stated explicitly in law until 1845, capital punishment was still allowed for treason, as seen in a few executions under Catherine II and famously in the execution of five Decembrist rebels in 1825. When capital punishment was finally presented systematically in the 1845 Criminal Code under the conservative Nicholas I (r. 1825–1855), it was limited only to attacks on the tsar himself, his family, and the state; all other crimes, including heresy, parricide, and murder, warranted exile or lesser punishments. Thus, the tsar epitomized the state and patrimonially protected his people from such a harsh punishment. Such an approach to the death penalty has a distinctly nonmodern feel, combining religious fervor, Enlightenment humanitarianism, and traditional Russian patriarchal ideology. The state continued with what one scholar calls a "comparatively lenient" use of punishment. Jonathan Daly, in a comparative study of punishment regimes in late nineteenth-century United States, Russia, and Europe, found that per capita Russia used execution, imprisonment, and other forms of punishment notably less than its peers.[16]

Russia's judicial practice into the nineteenth century, therefore, would seem to reflect an aversion to violence. But few of Pinker's driving forces for such a case were at play here, and those that were—Western norms of etiquette and Enlightenment humanitarian ideals—emerged late and complemented what was already going on. The pacifying impulse of commerce hardly played a role: Russia was a resource-poor society with a serf-based autarkic economy where the state exerted as much control over productive resources and economic exchange as possible. Therein probably lies the greatest difference between Russia's relationship to judicial violence and that of contemporary Europe: Russia relied upon a more complicated relationship to violence than Pinker's smooth path of decline.

Human and material resources were always the keys to state power in Russia and the state wielded violence intentionally to mobilize them. Russia's early modern state consolidated in the fourteenth and fifteenth centuries by conquering and absorbing neighbors; by the end of the fifteenth century it embarked on building a centralized state with a skeletal bureaucracy to govern new territories and to collect funds to support the growing cavalry army. Parallel to European states, Muscovy's claims on resources continuously expanded, in part because of modernization of the military into a gunpowder-armed cavalry army and, eventually, a European-style standing army, as well as because of imperial expansion. Empire required greater resources, and also provided them. By the end of the seventeenth century a skeletal network of fortresses stretching from European Russia to the Pacific solidified Russian tax-collecting authority over Siberia's fur-rich native tribes; conquests of Kazan (1552) and Astrakhan (1556) on the Volga expanded transit trade and opened the door to a slow but inexorable push across the steppe toward the Black and Caspian Seas and the Caucasus. By the end of the eighteenth century Russia was a major European geopolitical power, having captured the Black Sea littoral from the Ottoman Empire and dismembered Poland, bringing Ukrainian and Belorussian lands under Russian control. The only way all this success was possible was by a single-minded pursuit and control of resources, natural and human, to staff and equip the armies, support the elites, and maintain the bureaucracy of empire.

Pursuing such a policy produced a multisided approach to violence. In contrast to the preceding discussion of seemingly less violence in the criminal law, one can cite many ways in which Russia was a violent state and society. Take torture, for example. Russia borrowed some aspects of the revived Roman law that spread across Europe in the sixteenth century, including judicial torture. European criminal codes such as the Habsburg 1532 *Carolina* surrounded the use of torture with limitations (witnesses, doctors, limitation on sessions, requirement that the tortured sign his confession the next day, etc.).[17] Russia, however, lacked Europe's jurisprudential heritage; it had no guilds of lawyers or notaries, no law schools or seminaries, no legacy of Roman law or canon law, no university law faculties to turn to for expert advice (as the *Carolina* prescribed). Russia's criminal law mentioned torture only in passing, spelling out no limitations. Case law reveals that there was a de facto limit of three torture sessions in cases below highest crime, but with treason, heresy, and witchcraft, torture was used without bound. Here, the Russian criminal court was a violent place indeed.[18]

It was not, however, a medieval torture chamber of the sort that Pinker so macabrely (and inaccurately) details. Russian courts did not use arcane instruments of torture, only flogging in strappado position. Pain could be increased with the placing of weights on the body; fire was used in the most serious cases. Muscovite torture was not elaborate and mechanical, but suited for the task.

Over the sixteenth and seventeenth centuries the state moved to control peasant mobility; about half of its peasants were landlords' serfs and the others were tied to their villages in areas too infertile to support gentry. Such forced immobility helped the state by providing a labor force for the cavalry army and military elite and by making taxation easier. Violence was endemic in serfdom and peasant justice. The exile system, also a state creation, was brutal and often deadly. And the state continued to wield violence after the 1740s prohibition on the death penalty when and where it needed to: it routinely declared martial law (replete with corporal and capital punishment) on the Caucasus, steppe, and Central Asian borderlands to put down banditry, disorder, and opposition.[19]

Society more broadly shows the same mixed picture. The Russian nobility and merchant class were absorbing European etiquette and Enlightenment values, and several imperial elites—Ukrainian noblemen and Cossacks, Polish noblemen, Baltic German Junkers—came into the empire already European in culture. But Russian nobles also fell for the fashion of dueling in the late eighteenth and early nineteenth centuries in defiance of repeated edicts. Furthermore, literacy and European values that might have encouraged a decline of violence according to Pinker were not disseminated to the mass of the population, who remained bound to peasant communes and customary law even after the emancipation of 1861 and a judicial reform that provided jury courts for the higher social ranks (1864). Furthermore, maintaining the imperial governing strategy of tolerating difference left many communities devoid of schools, public services, literacy, urbanization, and a more differentiated economy. Only very late in the nineteenth century did the state attempt Russification to create some uniformity across the empire in language, education, and culture; only a few decades after mid-nineteenth-century reforms did industrialization, urbanization, transportation networks, and regional economic development expand, producing some of the softening effects (literacy, education, reason, commercial exchange) that Pinker cites. These processes were abruptly ended by the 1917 revolution, with effects evident today: Pinker observes that Russia and Eastern Europe today constitute a more violent periphery outside the core European area,[20] and in the twentieth century Russia suffered under a utopian ideology that wreaked unimaginable pain on the Soviet people.

The red thread uniting these disparate relationships to violence is the drive to mobilize resources. To ensure its survival the Russian state single-mindedly controlled violence among individuals and groups, using the criminal law and litigations over honor. It garnered labor power by preferring exile over execution. It carried out executions swiftly to assert the tsar's power, but had neither time nor resources or cultural inspiration to stage theatrical rituals. To keep up with European geopolitical rivals it forcibly Europeanized the nobility and educated classes, but it maintained serfdom for economic gain and political stability. Its "politics of difference" imperial policy intervened little in daily life for its many and diverse colonial subjects, ensuring stability but abandoning many to harsh customary discipline. The state rationally deployed or minimized violence to maximize its human resources as a strategic choice.

These reflections on the role of violence in Russia's early modern criminal law suggest that different states assess the utility of violence differently and use or limit it as it suits them. Just as Pinker himself notes that geographical isolation and poverty inhibit a decline in societal violence, a single-minded pursuit of limited resources pushed Russia to deploy violence in myriad ways, never approaching a steady march of decline. This messy, contingent outcome is the stuff of history.

Nancy Shields Kollmann is William H. Bonsall Professor in History at Stanford University. Her recent works include Crime and Punishment in Early Modern Russia *(2012) and* The Russian Empire, 1450–1801 *(2017).*

Notes

1. On state-building, see Charles Tilly and Gabriel Ardant, eds., *The Formation of National States in Western Europe* (Princeton, NJ: Princeton University Press, 1975). On etiquette: Norbert Elias, *The Civilizing Process,* 2 vols. (New York: Urizen Books,

1978–1982). On crime rates: Pieter Spierenburg, *The Spectacle of Suffering: Executions and the Evolution of Repression, From a Preindustrial Metropolis to the European Experience* (Cambridge: Cambridge University Press, 1984); Richard van Dülmen, *Theatre of Horror: Crime and Punishment in Early Modern Germany*, trans. Elisabeth Neu (Cambridge: Polity Press, 1990); Peter Linebaugh, *The London Hanged: Crime and Civil Society in the Eighteenth Century* (Cambridge: Cambridge University Press, 1992).

2. Steven Pinker, *The Better Angels of Our Nature: Why Violence Has Declined* (New York: Viking, 2011), 306.

3. Nancy Shields Kollmann, *Crime and Punishment in Early Modern Russia* (Cambridge: Cambridge University Press, 2012).

4. Marshall Poe, *"A People Born to Slavery": Russia in Early Modern European Ethnography, 1476–1748* (Ithaca, NY: Cornell University Press, 2000); Larry Wolff, *Inventing Eastern Europe: The Map of Civilization on the Mind of the Enlightenment* (Stanford, CA: Stanford University Press, 1994).

5. Michel Foucault, *Discipline and Punish: The Birth of the Prison*, trans. Alan Sheridan (New York: Vintage Books, 1979).

6. On stability in the elite: Kollmann, *Crime and Punishment*, 303–355. On honor litigation: Nancy Shields Kollmann, *By Honor Bound: State and Society in Early Modern Russia* (Ithaca, NY: Cornell University Press, 1999). On the Petrine law on dueling: Kollmann, *Crime and Punishment*, 406.

7. Nancy Shields Kollmann, *The Russian Empire, 1450–1801* (Oxford: Oxford University Press, 2017), 1–14.

8. Kollmann, *Crime and Punishment*, 94–112.

9. On forcible conversion: Kollmann, *Russian Empire*, 262–263, 397–402. On less violent religious rhetoric: Kollmann, *Crime and Punishment*, 424–425. On moral philosophy: Elise Kimerling Wirtschafter, *Religion and Enlightenment in Catherinian Russia: The Teachings of Metropolitan Platon* (DeKalb: Northern Illinois University Press, 2013).

10. On judicial expertise: Kollmann, *Crime and Punishment*, 47–73. On the Tunguz case: ibid., 203.

11. Ibid., 157–176.

12. Ibid., 241–257.

13. The horrific punishment of burning heretics inside wooded cages stuffed with incendiary material is recorded since the fifteenth century; the rebel Stepan Razin was quartered in 1671 and his body parts displayed on pikes for over a year.

14. Kollmann, *Crime and Punishment*, 380–415; Nancy Kollmann, "Pictures at an Execution: Johann Georg Korb's 'Execution of the Strel'tsy,'" in *Dubitando: Studies in History and Culture in Honor of Donald Ostrowski*, ed. Brian Boeck, Russell E. Martin, and Daniel Rowland (Bloomington, IN: Slavica Publishers, 2012), 399–407.

15. Abby M. Schrader, *Languages of the Lash: Corporal Punishment and Identity in Imperial Russia* (DeKalb: Northern Illinois University Press, 2002).

16. Jonathan Daly, "Russian Punishments in the European Mirror," in *Russia in the European Context 1789–1914: A Member of the Family*, ed. Michael Melancon (New York: Palgrave Macmillan, 2005), 161–88, here 176.

17. *Carolina*, arts. 18, 25–44, 54–56; see John H. Langbein, *Prosecuting Crime in the Renaissance: England, Germany, France* (Cambridge, MA: Harvard University Press, 1974), 272–283.

18. On revival of Roman law: Langbein, *Prosecuting Crime.* On judicial torture in Russia: Kollmann, *Crime and Punishment,* 133–156; Valerie A. Kivelson, *Desperate Magic: The Moral Economy of Witchcraft in Seventeenth-Century Russia* (Ithaca, NY: Cornell University Press, 2013).
19. John LeDonne, "Civilians under Military Justice during the Reign of Nicholas I," *Canadian-American Slavic Studies* 7 (1973): 171–187.
20. Pinker, *Better Angels,* 89, 229.

Chapter 5

Whitewashing History

Pinker's (Mis)Representation of the Enlightenment and Violence

Philip Dwyer

One of the cornerstones of Pinker's thesis explaining why violence has declined in the West is to be found in chapter 4, titled "The Humanitarian Revolution." There are two threads to Pinker's argument. The first is that people began to question the validity of "institutionalized violence"— by which he means human sacrifice, torture, and the persecution of heretics and witches—and to demand that that kind of violence be abolished. The second strand is that this thinking was "propelled by a change in sensibilities," by which he means that people (or at least Westerners) began to *sympathize* (his italics) with others, and were "no longer indifferent to their suffering."[1] This change in sensibilities took place from 1700 onward, and coincided with the advent of what Pinker calls the age of reason, a dated term for the Enlightenment, a movement that placed "life and happiness at the center of values," and that had "a sudden impact on Western life" in the second half of the eighteenth century.

Pinker likes to make bold statements. The Enlightenment led to: the elimination of capital and corporal punishments; a severe curtailment of government violence against "subjects"; the abolition of slavery (by which he means the abolition of the Atlantic slave trade); and people losing their "thirst for cruelty." Most readers would accept these assertions at face value.

Like all polemicists bent on proving a point, there is just enough truth to lend them credibility. But historians are a skeptical lot and are trained to question such bold statements. When we start to unpick them, Pinker's arguments begin to unravel. For a start, the central tenet of Pinker's thesis, as Sara Butler has pointed out in her chapter in this volume, is wrapped in a portrayal of Europe's past as ultraviolent and irrational. Without that juxtaposition, Pinker's argument about a decline in violence is untenable. Similarly, the complement to this violent portrayal of an extremely violent past—the creation of an enlightened, rational society in which "happiness" is at the center of our values—lacks historical grounding. Pinker has reduced the historical narrative to a crude dichotomy: before the Enlightenment, the world was superstitious, cruel, and violent; after the Enlightenment, the world was rational and more peaceful. In doing so, he reduces violence to a fairly simplistic concept; all violence can be equated with irrationality, unreason, and ignorance. History is never as straightforward as Pinker would have his readers believe, and violence is a much more complex notion that is often driven not by superstition or unreason, but perfectly "rational" motives. There are, therefore, a number of points that I would take issue with in this view of history and the Enlightenment.

The Enlightenment, Empathy, and the Reduction of Violence

It is true that the period in history known as the Enlightenment, roughly from the end of the seventeenth to the beginning of the nineteenth century, is a watershed moment in the history of Western civilization. It is during that time that many of the institutions, attitudes, and ideas that helped create the modern world took shape. We see the emergence of human rights with the American Declaration of Independence in 1776 and the French Declaration of the Rights of Man in 1789; both documents were to have an enormous influence on the development of world politics, not least of which was the development of democracy, something that Pinker argues made violence unnecessary.[2] Part of the invention of human rights was the development of empathy, which led to a revolution in the ways in which humans interacted with one another. More than empathy, however, Pinker believes, à la Norbert Elias and the civilizing process, that it was the development of self-control that led to a "thirty-fold drop" in violence from the medieval and early modern worlds.

Although empathy is a twentieth-century term, it is hardly credible to think that people in past societies did not empathize with or were indifferent to the victims of violence, or that they did not possess self-control. Pinker's argument is that "sympathy" and self-control were a corollary of the Enlightenment and "reason" and that they magically appeared in the second half of the eighteenth century. Anyone familiar with history, however, will tell you that people have always been genuinely concerned and shocked by violence, while those who have critiqued Elias in the past have argued that self-restraint was practiced by lower social orders for centuries.[3] Empathy has always been present in varying degrees and forms. Aztec mothers cried when their children were given up to sacrifice; medieval people were shocked by torture; not everyone who attended a public execution did so to delight in the suffering of the victim. There were of course different sensibilities, but the point is that empathy has always existed.

In a short work on the origins of human rights in the eighteenth century, Lynn Hunt has argued that there is a correlation between empathy and our ability to imagine other cultural experiences. She believes that increased empathy is linked to the rise of the epistolary novel in the second half of the eighteenth century—an assertion she admits is difficult to prove or measure.[4] Pinker largely adopts Hunt's arguments, reiterating that the increase in secular books and literacy rates helped set off the humanitarian revolution,[5] although his is a somewhat simplistic interpretation of a complicated and nuanced argument that has already elicited a good deal of discussion since Hunt's work appeared in 2009. For example, one could just as easily argue that heightened novel reading was more a consequence than a cause of feelings of equality and sympathy.[6] Moreover, the argument cuts both ways; that is, the novel might encourage empathy, but it may also encourage its opposite, hatred through the ability to imagine violence. That in turn might predispose people toward committing it. This is why so much research has been done on the impact of violence on the screen, big and small, on children. Finally, can we ever really "feel" the pain of others? It is a question Elaine Scarry posed in the 1980s; she did not believe we could.[7] It adds an additional layer to the discussions that are missing in Pinker and to a lesser extent in Hunt.

The so-called rise of empathy, in other words, might explain why some people donate to starving children in the developing world, but it falls short of understanding why a number of genocides were committed in the twentieth century, or why "ordinary" people are able to kill and torture. I would go so far as to argue that in collective settings mass killings and torture are not about loss of self-control or lack of empathy; rather, they are about identification with one's group to the detriment of another. The uses of torture by the French during the Algerian War of Independence (1954–1962), and more recently by Americans during the war in Iraq, are cases in point.[8] People placed in extraordinary circumstances are more than capable of committing atrocities, especially if they think they are acting for a higher good. This is as valid a statement of people's behavior today as it is for past centuries.

Do Ideas Drive History?

The notion of empathy is important for understanding what comes next in Pinker's argument. He makes a causal link between the Enlightenment and the changes in attitude to certain kinds of violence, such as torture and public executions. In fact, Pinker takes Hunt's thesis one step further. He contends that the reason so many violent institutions succumbed within a short space of time was that they were slain by a "coherent philosophy" that emerged during the Enlightenment.[9]

In talking about the Enlightenment, Pinker touches on the question of whether ideas move history or whether ideas simply reflect and encapsulate contemporary social and political trends. It is a question I used to pose to my undergraduate students when teaching the origins of the French Revolution, a question with which historians have grappled for generations: does a "revolution of the mind" necessarily have to precede a revolution in act?[10] The answer is that a revolution without ideas is simply a revolt. This is not the same as saying, however, that ideas drove people to revolution, or reform, for that matter. For Pinker, however, the answer is clear: ideas move history and reduce violence.[11] In order to arrive at that conclusion, he posits that the disappearance of the opposite of "reason," that is, ignorance and superstition, such as the ideas that "gods demand sacrifices, witches cast spells, heretics go to hell, Jews poison wells, animals are insensate, children are possessed, Africans are brutish, and kings rule by divine right," undermines the rationale for violence.[12]

There are two problems with this kind of thinking. The first is the difficulty, if not the impossibility, of demonstrating a causal link between reading, thinking, and action. This is where Pinker's obliviousness to history and its methodologies come into play. To assume that one event or idea necessarily leads to another completely underestimates the complexity of the historical process; in this particular instance, of reading and the internalization process.[13] As two leading lights on the origins of the French Revolution, Roger Chartier and Keith Baker, have pointed out, discourses do not necessarily shape practices.[14] All sorts of other factors have to be taken into account.

The second problem with thinking that the Enlightenment was responsible for a decline in violence is the assumption that humanist reformers were motivated by concern over the suffering of their fellow human beings. That was not always the case; motives appear to have been far more practical and far less idealistic than Pinker allows for. Let me focus on one example: public executions. The right of the state to use violence, and in some instances extreme forms of violence like breaking on the wheel and burning at the stake, was never really called into question. Neither apparently did the taste for viewing public executions and displayed bodies wane during this period.[15] On the contrary, there is some evidence to suggest that executions were popular across all social classes well into the nineteenth century.[16] Large crowds in the tens of thousands would regularly turn out to see public executions in London right up until they were finally banned in 1868—and not in 1783, as Pinker claims.[17]

What was questioned, and gave rise to a great deal of concern among the ruling elites, was the behavior and attitudes of the populace, as well as a belief that the condemned were no longer abiding by the preordained rituals. English observers considered the crowds that gathered to watch hangings to be far too turbulent and far too merry, but it was the behavior of the crowd along the processional route in London from Newgate prison to Tyburn, the traditional site of public executions, that was particularly concerning. The civil authorities feared that they had lost control of the process. It was one of the reasons why in 1783, public hangings were relocated from Tyburn to the front of Newgate prison. It was thus hoped that by containing the size of the crowd, public order would be restored. That was not to be; there were recurring incidents of crowd misbehavior. In 1849, Charles Dickens wrote to the *Times* after witnessing the hanging of Frederik and Maria Manning, railing not against the death penalty but rather against "the wickedness and levity of the immense crowd."[18]

Other examples across Europe could be given, but the point is that reform was born of a complicated mixture of fear of the rabble at a time when the revolutionary potential of the mob was very much alive, and a shifting of cultural values: crowds had become indifferent to the spectacle of violence; put another way, violence in "progressive" societies no longer resulted in the required pedagogical outcome. This is not to say that crowds had lost interest in visible acts of brutality during the nineteenth century. On the contrary, they were still very much fascinated by displays of violence. Disgust among the elites at the sight and smell of mutilated bodies or public executions were only ever secondary considerations. Eventually, authorities banned public executions in Western Europe during the second half of the nineteenth century, not because they were inhumane—although that thought was certainly there—but because they no longer represented an edifying enough spectacle to the people who witnessed them.

The Paradox of the Enlightenment

Pinker admits to the unevenness of the progress, but what has escaped his attention is the overriding paradox, to use Lynn Hunt's phrase, between the emergence of the language of human rights during the American and French Revolutions and the extraordinary violence wrought on civilians by opposing ideological parties.[19] The great paradox is that human rights could not have occurred without violent revolution, including the American Revolution, which recent research has shown to be far more ferocious than had previously been thought.[20] In other words, violence drove change.

There are a number of other paradoxes that are worth highlighting and that permeated the eighteenth and early nineteenth centuries. At the same time that Enlightenment values were coming into their own, the English Parliament increased the number of crimes punishable by death fivefold, from about 50 in 1688 to about 240 in 1820.[21] Of course, many were able to avoid execution so that the number that occurred between 1770 and

1830 declined to a "relatively modest" seven thousand. But here is the rub. Why the number of executions actually dropped around the middle of the seventeenth century and stayed that way for most of the eighteenth is one of the biggest mysteries in English penal history. Historians have put forth a number of suggestions but none of them is particularly conclusive, because we simply do not know. It is thus a little presumptuous of Pinker, if not misleading, to cut a swathe through this kind of historical dilemma, as if it had not taxed the minds of a number of eminent historians, and to present a simplistic response—it must be the Enlightenment—which serves merely to suit his agenda.

Another paradox is that racism as a pseudoscientific ideology really only came into its own in the nineteenth century, at about the same time as slavery was abolished in Europe. Moreover, this was a period, that is, the decades after 1760, when the slave trade reached a peak. The French slave trade actually spiked in the years 1783–1792/3, only to be interrupted by the outbreak of war between revolutionary France and the rest of Europe.[22] It is, therefore, difficult to reconcile the values of the Enlightenment, as they were understood and practiced in Europe, with colonialism and Europe's excessively violent domination of the non-European world. More importantly, though, it is possible to question the traditional narrative of the abolition of the slave trade as a unique result of the Enlightenment or humanitarian movement. A recent analysis of various cases of *abolition* around the world reveals the extent to which other motives, often masked as humanitarianism, played a role.[23] The British naval campaign against slavery from the mid-nineteenth century was motivated by a desire to enforce abolition, yes, but was also driven by the British desire to control the seas, as well as a personal desire on the part of many navy captains for prize money. Again, the connections between Enlightenment values and the invention of human rights are much more complex than Pinker has allowed for. People, as I am sure Pinker would admit, can be both rational and irrational (or spiritual), can be both practical and idealistic, and can be both concerned for and indifferent to the fate of others. In other words, people are motivated by somewhat contradictory impulses, but change can come about only by a combination of complex historical forces, most of which Pinker seems to ignore.

Reason and Violence in History

The last point I would like to make concerns Pinker's statement that today "the Enlightenment is often mentioned with a sneer."[24] One might think that this is quibbling, that out of a 700-page book it is unfair to pick up on a small detail, but I think it goes to the heart of how Pinker's mind works. After having set up a before and after paradigm turning on the Enlightenment, Pinker then declares that everyone from the Left to theoconservatives, passing over moderate secularists, has disparaged the Enlightenment, resulting in a "colossal amnesia and ingratitude," only possible because of the "natural whitewashing of history."[25] In other words, we (the reader or the historian, it is not clear) have simply forgotten just how violent the past was and have equally forgotten just how important the Enlightenment was in bringing about a peaceful change.

Pinker does not explicitly say so, but it is possible that his general "disparagement" is a reference to the debates that took place in the 1970s–1990s that emerged out of the Frankfurt School. Spearheaded by the likes of Max Horkheimer and Theodor Adorno, they argued that the Enlightenment was not the solution to the problems of modern society, but rather its source.[26] To put their argument succinctly, the totalitarianism of the twentieth century was the result of rationalism taken to its extreme, so that the Enlightenment led to the Holocaust. Zygmunt Baumann is probably the best-known proponent of the thesis that the Holocaust was deeply rooted in modern, Western civilization, and that genocide was intertwined with democracy.[27]

This argument has influenced the way people think about the Enlightenment, which is not to say that scholars have dismissed it or "sneer" at it. In the last decade or two, the Enlightenment has been examined from all sorts of different perspectives—gender, the role of women, science, race, sexuality, as well as geographical foci—leaving us with a far more complex view of it.[28] Dan Edelstein, for example, has recently argued that the Terror during the French Revolution emerged from Enlightenment ideas—not the same thing as arguing that the Enlightenment is to blame for the Terror—singling out the tradition of what he calls "natural law" or "natural rights," the belief that certain rights are inherent by virtue of human nature.[29]

All of these debates seem to have gone over Pinker's head, leaving his readers with the idea of a monolithic Enlightenment that historians have long since discarded.[30] Not surprisingly, because it is a theoretical-historical rather than an empirical argument, Pinker fails to mention the powerful illiberal current in Enlightenment thinking. That illiberal current includes, in the West at least, the Jacobins, the Bolsheviks, and the Nazis, all political ideologies that at their core believed humans and human society could be improved through violent means. They all not only advocated but also practiced violence in a methodical way to bring about revolutionary change in society.

Pinker rejects these ideologies as "counter-Enlightenment utopianism."[31] He cannot countenance the idea, for example, that there was a link between the "invention of reason" and the industrial extermination of people carried out by the Nazis, because for him violence is necessarily irrational. That is, I would argue, to misunderstand the fundamental nature of violence. Violence serves a purpose and a function, no matter how "irrational" or "barbaric" or "savage" an act might appear to the outside observer. This is as much the case today as it was in the past. Take as an example rape in warfare, which has become a systematic strategy in some modern theaters of war. In Mozambique, soldiers often force local men to watch them raping women; the ritual mutilation of victims is carried out by cutting off noses, breasts, penises, and so on; parents are forced to maim or kill their children, to cook and eat them prior to their own execution.[32] These are all "rational" and calculated techniques designed to instill terror into populations, thereby preventing them from engaging in organized resistance. At the heart of attempts to understand human motivation behind violence is a question that can be asked of all political ideologies that descend into terror: what makes ordinary people choose violence?[33] Of course the process is complicated; it is not just about understanding rhetoric and ideas, but also about placing them in their social and political context.

Getting the History Right

Perhaps historians would be more receptive of Pinker's claims if he managed to get most of his history right. It is not merely that he makes mistakes—all of us do—but rather that he makes spurious claims based on at best a misinterpretation, or at worst, a complete misunderstanding, of history. I present three examples; two are relatively straightforward, but the third is complicated and has to do (again) with the manner in which Pinker engages—or rather does not engage—with history. First, his use of sources can only be described as eccentric. For example, in one paragraph discussing the power of despots to kill, Pinker cites the story of King Solomon in the Bible, Scheherazade from the *Thousand and One Nights,* an anecdote about Narasimhadev I of India from the thirteenth century, and Dr. Seuss.[34] This apparent inability to distinguish between fact and fiction, legend and reality, examples of which are dotted throughout the book, cannot serve as a substitute for concrete historical evidence. This kind of mishmash would not pass muster in an undergraduate essay, so why should we accept it from Pinker?

Second, Pinker's figures for violent deaths are sometimes close to what historians generally agree on, but usually on the high and sometimes on the very high end of estimates, and they are presented with an assurance that belies the complexity of the events they represent. The most concerning aspect of these figures is that Pinker simply does not engage with specialists in the field; even when he does, he seems to ignore their findings. For example, Pinker claims that 350,000 died during the Spanish Inquisition. This is wrong: the historiography of the last 20 years shows the Inquisition was not as punitive as was once thought, so that we now think the figure was probably fewer than 10,000 deaths.[35] That figure has been suggested by Joseph Pérez in *The Spanish Inquisition.* What is odd about this is that Pinker actually cites Pérez elsewhere in his book, which leads one to think that Pinker either missed or ignored the figure in question, or he is cherry-picking and chose instead another, higher estimate simply because it supported his theory.

This careless use of statistics shows up starkly in his discussion of the French Revolutionary and Napoleonic Wars, my area of specialty. Pinker claims the wars resulted in as many as four million deaths, earning a spot on his list of 21 worst things people have ever done to each other.[36] Pinker actually conflates the French Revolutionary and Napoleonic Wars, but let's not quibble. It is a figure sometimes cited by historians, but at best it is a guesstimate; no one has ever tried to count the number of deaths resulting from the wars. There are problems of geography—the wars raged from Andalucía in Spain to the region of Moscow, from Amsterdam to the Illyrian coast, and everything in between—without taking into account the global scale of the wars. There are also problems around the lack of documentation. It is simply not possible to get accurate figures for the numbers of men who died in skirmishes or battles—those killed in the field, or who later died of their wounds—let alone the number of civilians who died, either directly or indirectly from disease and starvation, as a consequence of the wars. As a result, figures for civilian deaths among historians vary wildly, from between 750,000 and 5 million people.[37] It might be less than the lowest estimate or more than the highest; we simply do not know. A few regional studies have been done. The French presence in Calabria, in southern Italy, led to a diminution of 21,000 people out of an estimated population of a little more than 800,000.[38] That is about 2 to 3 percent of the population, but we do not know how many died and how many simply fled a region of intense violence. Recent studies of the impact of the war in Spain between 1808 and 1814 have estimated the total number of deaths at between 560,000 and 885,000 people (out of a population of 10 million), that is, between 5 and 8 percent of the population, including death by disease and famine.[39] But Calabria and Spain are the two regions hardest hit by the wars and we cannot extrapolate from there to the rest of Europe, where figures would have varied enormously from region to region.

As for military deaths, we have a reasonably accurate figure for the number of casualties among French troops. Of the two million men (French and foreign) conscripted in Napoleon's *Grande Armée* between 1803 and 1814, probably around 900,000 men (and some women) died, the majority not on the battlefield but as a result of their wounds or of disease.[40] According to the most accurate assessment to date, the total number of French troops who died between 1798 and 1815 is estimated at around 1.7 million men.[41] But, we cannot know the casualties for the other European combatant armies because no one has counted them. Nor do we know with any degree of accuracy what percentage of the French male population the casualties represent. One historian cites the figure of 38 percent of French males born between 1790 and 1795 who died during the wars; another 20 percent.[42] In 1806, the total population of France, without the territories incorporated into the empire, was probably just over 29 million. The death toll therefore was probably 5.8 percent of the total population. Compare this to the number of French males born between 1891 and 1894 who fell during

World War I: 14 percent, according to one historian, 25 percent according to another.[43] Even when historians do know roughly how many died in a conflict, they will disagree about how to interpret those figures.

Conclusion

Does this kind of criticism around history and the numbers of dead discredit Pinker or detract from his overall thesis? I would argue that it does, largely because it highlights the difficulties historians routinely face when trying to decide what constitutes reliable historical evidence, especially when the evidence is sparse or partial. Pinker's thesis ultimately fails because he has a limited depth of understanding of history and historical methodology. In effect, Pinker wants history to neatly fit his thesis. Without an intimate knowledge of history, his work can never be more than a collection of generalizations based upon flawed notions of who people were and why they acted the way they did. He constantly exaggerates the violence of the past in order to support his claim that previous centuries were, statistically speaking, much more violent than the present. He almost never, if at all, questions the accuracy or the nature of the sources he uses. We therefore end up with a problematic hypothesis, backed by somewhat doubtful empirical data, and an even more problematic theory. I am referring to Norbert Elias's the "civilizing process," upon which other contributors in this volume elaborate. The point worth underlining here is that the past is never a linear progression and that life was not always "nasty, brutish, and short." If any "whitewashing" is going on, it is not that we, as professional historians, have forgotten the violence of the past, but that Pinker, as amateur historian, has failed to seriously engage with our work.

Philip Dwyer is Professor of History and founding Director of the Study for the History of Violence at the University of Newcastle, Australia. He has written on the Revolutionary and Napoleonic Wars, memoirs, violence, and colonialism. He is the general editor (with Joy Damousi) of the four-volume Cambridge World History of Violence, *forthcoming with Cambridge University Press.*

Notes

1. Steven Pinker, *The Better Angels of Our Nature: Why Violence Has Declined* (New York: Allen Lane, 2011), 133.
2. David Armitage, *The Declaration of Independence: A Global History* (Cambridge, MA: Harvard University Press, 2007).
3. For empathy, see the review of Pinker by Hannah Skoda in http://ideas nowandthen.blogspot.com.au/. For self-restraint, see Dennis Smith, *Norbert Elias and Modern Social Theory* (London: Sage, 2001), 161–166.

4. Lynn Hunt, *Inventing Human Rights: A History* (New York: W. W. Norton, 2007), 32.
5. Pinker, *Better Angels,* 172–177.
6. Gordon S. Wood, "Natural, Equal, Universal," *New York Times,* 8 April 2007.
7. Elaine Scarry, *The Body in Pain: The Making and Unmaking of the World* (New York: Oxford University Press, 1985).
8. Marnia Lazreg, *Torture and the Twilight of Empire: From Algiers to Baghdad* (Princeton, NJ: Princeton University Press, 2007).
9. Pinker, *Better Angels,* 180, 183.
10. Robert Darnton, "An Enlightened Revolution?," *New York Review of Books* (24 October 1991), 33–36, put the question a little differently: "How did the cultural system of the Old Regime contribute to the political explosion of 1789?"; Roger Chartier, *Les origines culturelles de la Révolution française* (Paris: Seuil, 1990), 86–115, posed the question differently again: "Do books make revolutions?"
11. Pinker, *Better Angels,* 477.
12. Ibid., 645.
13. Timothy Tackett, *The Coming of the Terror in the French Revolution* (Cambridge, MA: Belknap Press, 2015), 29–30, 33–38.
14. Roger Chartier, "The Chimera of the Origin: Archaeology, Cultural History, and the French Revolution," in *Foucault and the Writing of History,* ed. Jan Goldstein (Oxford: Blackwell, 1994), 167–186, here 175–177.
15. See Richard J. Evans, *Rituals of Retribution: Capital Punishment in Germany, 1600–1987* (London: Penguin, 1996), 135, 214, 193–196, 225–226; and Mark Hewitson, *Absolute War: Violence and Mass Warfare in the German Lands, 1792–1820* (Oxford: Oxford University Press, 2017), 128–131.
16. Matthew White, "'Rogues of the Meaner Sort'? Old Bailey Executions and the Crowd in the Early Nineteenth Century," *The London Journal* 33, no. 2 (2008): 135–153.
17. Pinker, *Better Angels,* 149.
18. *Times,* 13 November 1849. My thanks to Una McIlvenna for pointing this out.
19. Lynn Hunt, "The Paradoxical Origins of Human Rights," in *Human Rights and Revolutions,* ed. Jeffrey N. Wasserstrom, Lynn Hunt, and Marilyn B. Young (Lanham, MD: Rowman and Littlefield, 2007), 3–17; Hunt, *Inventing Human Rights,* 32, 35–58.
20. Holger Hoock, *Scars of Independence: America's Violent Birth* (New York: Crown Publishing, 2017).
21. Simon Devereaux, "The Promulgation of the Statutes in Late Hanoverian Britain," in *The British and Their Laws in the Eighteenth Century,* ed. David Lemmings (Woodbridge, UK: Boydell Press, 2005), 80–101, here 85–86; James Sharpe, *A Fiery & Furious People: A History of Violence in England* (New York: Random House, 2016), 393, 394, 396.
22. James A. Rawley, with Stephen D. Behrendt, *The Transatlantic Slave Trade: A History* (Lincoln: University of Nebraska Press, 2005), 15, 111, 113.
23. Hideaki Suzuki, "Abolitions as a Global Experience: An Introduction," in *Abolitions as a Global Experience,* ed. Hideaki Suzuki (Singapore: NUS Press, 2015), 1–24, here 7–9.
24. Pinker, *Better Angels,* 133.
25. Ibid.

26. A good summary of the anti-Enlightenment trend is in Hunt, "The Paradoxical Origins of Human Rights," 4–5.
27. Zygmunt Bauman, *Modernity and the Holocaust* (Cambridge: Polity Press, 1990). For a critique of this approach see, Marsha Healy, "The Holocaust, Modernity and the Enlightenment," *Res Publica* 3, no. 1 (1997): 35–59.
28. See Charles W. J. Withers, *Placing the Enlightenment: Thinking Geographically about the Age of Reason* (Chicago: University of Chicago Press, 2007), 1–6, for an overview of recent scholarly trends.
29. Dan Edelstein, *The Terror of Natural Right: Republicanism, the Cult of Nature, and the French Revolution* (Chicago: University of Chicago Press, 2009), 127–169. See also the critique by Annie Jourdan (http://www.laviedesidees.fr/Le-mystere-de-la-Terreur.html), and Dan Edelstein's reply (http://www.laviedesidees.fr/La-Re publique-la-nature-et-le.html).
30. Withers, *Placing the Enlightenment*, 41.
31. Pinker, *Better Angels*, 207–208.
32. See, for example, K. B. Wilson, "Cults of Violence and Counter-Violence in Mozambique," *Journal of Southern African Studies* 18, no. 3 (September 1992): 527–582; and John Keane, *Violence and Democracy* (Cambridge: Cambridge University Press, 2004), 54–65.
33. The question has motivated books as diverse as Marisa Linton, *Choosing Terror: Virtue, Friendship, and Authenticity in the French Revolution* (Oxford: Oxford University Press, 2013), and Christopher R. Browning, *Ordinary Men: Reserve Police Battalion 101 and the Final Solution in Poland* (New York: HarperCollins, 1992).
34. Pinker, *Better Angels*, 159.
35. Joseph Pérez, *The Spanish Inquisition: A History* (New Haven, CT: Yale University Press, 2006), 173.
36. Pinker, *Better Angels*, figure 5–18, p. 230.
37. Charles J. Esdaile, *The Wars of Napoleon* (London: Longman, 1995), 300, estimates a figure of one million civilian losses.
38. Cited in Nicolas Cadet, "Violences de guerre et transmission de la mémoire des conflits à travers l'exemple de la campagne de Calabre de 1806–1807," *Annales historiques de la Révolution française* 348 (April–June 2007): 147–163, here 153.
39. Esteban Canales, "1808–1814: Démographie et guerre en Espagne," *Annales historiques de la Révolution française* 336 (April–June 2004): 37–52; Vicente Pérez Moreda, "Las crisis demográficas del periodo napoleónico en España," in *La guerra de Napoleón en España: Reacciones, imágenes, consecuencias*, ed. Emilio La Parra López (Madrid: Casa de Velázquez, 2010), 305–332.
40. Jacques Houdaille, "Le problème des pertes de la guerre," *Revue d'histoire moderne et contemporaine* 17 (1970): 411–423.
41. Jacques Houdaille, "Pertes de l'armée de terre sous l'empire," *Population* 27 (1972): 27–50.
42. Peter Browning, *The Changing Nature of Warfare: The Development of Land Warfare from 1792 to 1945* (Cambridge: Cambridge University Press, 2002), 45.
43. Colin S. Gray, *War, Peace and International Relations: An Introduction to Strategic History* (Abingdon, UK: Routledge, 2012), 37; David Gates, *Warfare in the Nineteenth Century* (Houndmills, UK: Palgrave, 2001), 55; John A. Lynn, "Nations in Arms 1763–815," in *The Cambridge Illustrated History of Warfare*, ed. Geoffrey Parker (New York: Cambridge University Press, 2005), 210.

Chapter 6

Assessing Violence in the Modern World

Richard Bessel

How are we to assess changing levels of violence in the modern world? The answer put forward by Canadian-born Harvard psychologist Steven Pinker is unambiguous: "Violence has been in decline over long stretches of history, and today we are probably living in the most peaceful moment of our species' time on earth."[1] In his widely read book *The Better Angels of Our Nature*, Pinker claims that its subject "may be the most important thing that has ever happened in human history. Believe it or not—and I know that most people do not—violence has declined over long stretches of time, and today we may be living in the most peaceable era in our species' existence."[2] The catalogue of horrors that disfigured the history of the twentieth century notwithstanding, Pinker argues that people are becoming less violent, not more:

> In sixteenth-century Paris, a popular form of entertainment was cat-burning, in which a cat was hoisted in a sling on a stage and slowly lowered into a fire . . . Today, such sadism would be unthinkable in most of the world. This change in sensibilities is just one example of perhaps the most important and most underappreciated trend in the human saga: Violence has been in decline over long stretches of history, and today we are probably living in the most peaceful moment of our species' time on earth.

> In the decade of Darfur and Iraq, and shortly after the century of Stalin, Hitler, and Mao, the claim that violence has been diminishing may seem somewhere between hallucinatory and obscene. Yet recent studies that seek to quantify the historical ebb and flow of violence point to exactly that con-

clusion . . . Conventional history has long shown that, in many ways, we have been getting kinder and gentler.[3]

Of course, that depends on who "we" are considered to be. Kindness and gentleness might be easier to exercise in contemporary Sweden or Japan than in Afghanistan or the Democratic Republic of the Congo. And evidence that there has been a "change in sensibilities"—and the evidence for this change is considerable[4]—is not necessarily evidence that violence itself has been diminishing (or, for that matter, increasing). However, what Pinker's argument and the contrasting assessments of people who continue to regard our era as "the most bloody era of human history" have in common is an intense, almost obsessive interest in violence as a historical topic. History, as Jörg Baberowski reminds us, is "a science that gives answers to questions of the present," not the past.[5] We tend to view history in terms of current concerns and preoccupations, and ours center around violence.

Measuring Violence: Homicide

As much of Pinker's argument rests on data concerning violent events, a useful place to begin assessing his argument is with what may seem the clearest indicator of levels of violence, and one that frequently is used by researchers aiming to measure and compare levels of violence, namely, homicide. Whereas many assaults never emerge in statistics of recorded crime,[6] and whereas rape within marriage has become a punishable offense and thus recorded as such only in recent decades (and even now only a tiny proportion of such offenses are prosecuted),[7] common sense may suggest that drawing conclusions from murder statistics should be straightforward. After all, corpses can be counted, and the tallies compared. Pieter Spierenburg, a leading scholar of homicide in early modern Europe, has observed:

> Most scholars working within this tradition [i.e., examining homicide with a primarily quantitative approach] consider the incidence of homicide as an indication for the level of violence in past societies. They follow criminological usage in taking as their measure the homicide rate, defined as the annual average of killings, over a specified period, per 100,000 population in a given area. A rise or a decline in this rate would mean that the society in question became respectively more or less violent.[8]

Spierenburg is of the opinion that, at least in Western countries, "the evidence really shows that we have become less violent, . . . and we know that they [murders] have declined very much in terms of rates per hundred thousand per year from the Middle Ages up to the present."[9]

Pinker essentially offers the same argument: "Homicide is the crime of choice for measurers of violence because regardless of how people of a distant culture conceptualize crime, a dead body is hard to define away, and it always arouses curiosity about who or what produced it. Records of homicide are therefore a more reliable index of violence than records of robbery, rape, or assault, and they usually (though not always) correlate with them."[10] He refers, for example, to Manuel Eisner's longitudinal estimates of homicide in England from the thirteenth through the twentieth centuries, based on coroners' inquests, court cases, and local records, as well as to J. S. Cockburn's "continuous data from the town [sic] of Kent between 1560 and 1985" to show that there was "a decline in annual homicide rates [that] is not small."[11] By combining data on "homicide rates in five Western European regions, 1300–2000," Eisner shows—and Pinker cites—similar declines in homicides per 100,000 people per year.[12] And when looking at what may be regarded as the most violent country in the contemporary West, Pinker notes that "the annual homicide rate in the United States at its recent worst—10.2 per 100,000 in 1980—was a quarter of the rate for Western Europe in 1450."[13]

But was the same thing being counted in 1980 as in 1450? In order to draw conclusions from the data we have about homicide, we need to be clear about what is being counted, who is doing the counting, and what the purposes of the data are. Even where the counting exercise may seem to be straightforward, that is, with regard to what appears the most obvious indicator of violent crime, homicide, some skepticism may be in order. Thus, before jumping to the conclusion that a rise or fall in the number of murders reported over time in a particular jurisdiction necessarily reflects a rise or fall in the level of violence, it is worth considering how a corpse becomes a murder case.

Here research by Howard Taylor on murder in England and Wales during the late nineteenth and twentieth centuries offers a revealing insight. Taylor observes that "the statistics of murder . . . for the period 1880 to 1966 kept to a cumulative average of 150 a year, . . . within a range of 20 percent either side of the average."[14] That is to say, over nearly nine decades, during which time the population of England and Wales roughly doubled,[15] the numbers of (reported) murders in England and Wales remained more or less constant. While "the traditional literature has sought to explain this largely by arguing that there occurred an 'English miracle' when crime diminished as the population rose," Taylor looked elsewhere, "arguing that the crime statistics largely reflected supply-side policies."[16] That is to say, the remarkable figures noted above reflected what was being counted as murder, and that was, in Taylor's view, a function of the public prosecution budget. According to Taylor, "because the discovery of a suspicious death and its subsequent investigation and prosecution could make a large dent in a police authority budget, the chances were that it would not be prosecuted as a murder."[17]

Obviously not all violent crime data may be affected in ways such as those stressed by Taylor, but doubts about the validity of prosecution statistics for the measurement of homicide are not exclusive to those for nineteenth- and twentieth-century England. For example, reflecting on homicide in early modern England, Spierenburg himself has stated baldly that "criminal prosecutions simply cannot be trusted as a source for the incidence of killing" and notes that "even more dramatic evidence comes from sixteenth-century Amsterdam," concluding "that criminal prosecutions constitute an inferior source for the construction of homicide."[18]

The problems posed by such data are not simply a consequence of the "inferior" quality of criminal prosecutions as a source for measuring trends in murder. There also is the problem that, due to advances in hygiene and medicine, people in developed countries are much less likely to die as a result of wounds, for example, from stabbings. The same violent physical act—thrusting a knife into another person—is far less likely to result in a death in, for example, twenty-first-century London than it was in fifteenth-century Florence. Roy Porter has observed that "early efforts to suture stab wounds, for example, resulted in a mortality of 50–60 percent, mostly due to infection, but by World War II, drawing on sulfa drugs and antibiotics, surgeons were able to open the heart without undue risk."[19]

Measuring Violence: War

These improvements have dramatically affected deaths from military campaigns. Until relatively recently, the majority of the deaths of soldiers as a result of combat were of men who died later of their wounds rather than being killed quickly on the battlefield. For example, data relating to deaths of French soldiers during the Revolutionary and Napoleonic Wars indicate that only a small proportion of the losses were of those who actually died in and during combat; many times more died subsequently from their wounds, while the majority—roughly two-thirds—died as a result of disease.[20] "François Vigo-Roussillon noted in his campaign diary for 28 Germinal Year V [17 April 1797], after the battle of Neumarck, that 'a large proportion of the wounded . . . perished in the woods because they were not evacuated and treated.'"[21] During the Franco-Prussian War, "the French amputated some 13,200 limbs, with 10,000 gangrene and fever deaths—a mortality rate of 76 percent."[22] These soldiers' present-day counterparts in the American armed forces who fought, for example, in Iraq and who were treated for wounds in well-equipped medical facilities very quickly after having been wounded, usually survived. Does that mean that the French Revolutionary Wars and the Franco-Prussian War were more violent than the American-led invasion of Iraq, where "far more soldiers are surviving even grievous injuries than in previous conflicts"[23] and thus the proportion that died was far lower?

This transformation is not something that suddenly materialized during the last decade. Already by the eve of World War I, despite the increasing destructiveness of weaponry to the human body, medical care on the battlefield was becoming more effective. According to an article on "The Blessings of Science on the Battlefield" published in the *Scientific American* at the end of 1913: "Military surgery, indeed, appears . . . to have undergone what may fairly be called a revolution since, say, the war of 1870. And the sum total of results in the contest between the agencies of death and the agencies of life is, in regard to recoveries from wounds not instantaneously fatal, that the average number of deaths in 1870 has been reduced by one half."[24] The improvements continued over the twentieth century, and today the "blessings of science on the battlefield" have reached levels unimaginable a century ago. In a recent article in the *British Medical Journal,* on "Lessons from the Battlefield," Anne Gulland observed that "a solider injured in Afghanistan or Iraq will get treatment that a pedestrian knocked down by a car on a high street in the United Kingdom could only dream of."[25]

The revolutionary development of military medical care is reflected in the changing relationship between the numbers of dead and wounded. According to the United States Department of Defense, as a result of Operation Iraqi Freedom there were 4,411 military deaths, of which 3,481 were soldiers killed in action and 930 (21.1%) died due to "nonhostile" causes.[26] The ratio of dead to wounded for American forces was roughly 1:7.4 (or about 1:8.9, if one strips away the 19 percent killed by nonhostile causes such as motor vehicle accidents). By contrast, among the German armed forces during World War I, the ratio of dead to wounded was roughly 1:2.36.[27] That is to say, the counterparts of many of those who a hundred years ago would have been counted among the dead more recently would have been among the wounded and would have survived their war. Another reflection of this transformation is the changing probability of a soldier dying in a particular conflict: even compared with America's Vietnam War, during the Iraq War the chances of a US soldier dying declined by more than five times, while the proportion of dead to wounded declined by roughly two-thirds.[28] The intensity of combat, and the relative levels of violence, therefore may not be reflected in the numbers of military dead that result, since so many soldiers in the late twentieth century survived wounds that would have killed their counterparts in earlier conflicts.

The wars fought by Western armies also have become less deadly for their soldiers because the proportion of military personnel involved directly in combat has fallen precipitously in recent decades. That is to say, as armies have become smaller (with the move away from large conscript armies and toward leaner, professional armed forces), a smaller proportion of those in uniform has been involved directly in the application of lethal violence. Logistics played an increasingly important role in war fighting over the twentieth century, with World War I marking a watershed as "the first true, modern war" in which millions of men had to be supplied with vast amounts of materiel, from ammunition to food.[29] However, it was with the West's wars of the late twentieth and early twenty-first centuries that the application of violence became the task of a relatively small minority of soldiers at war. For example, according to a 2002 study of postcombat syndromes among British soldiers over the course of the twentieth century, "the proportion involved in actual fighting fell over time as the numbers in combat-support roles has risen . . . of the First World War pensioners 73.4% [had been in combat], of the Second World War sample 52%, while only 19.8% of the Gulf War sample had seen action."[30] It was estimated that during America's Vietnam War, for every soldier in the field there were seven in support roles: "cooks, clerks, supply people, maintenance men, truck drivers, military po-licemen, entertainment personnel, headquarters' staffs and men running PXs."[31] Whether this means that the Vietnam War—which claimed the lives of more than three million people altogether—was somehow less violent than previous wars is an open question.

Changing Sensibilities toward Violence

Constructing arguments, as Pinker does, based on long-term trends in vi-olent crime (such as "the European homicide decline"[32]), or relative death tolls in wars,[33] thus is less straightforward than often assumed. This is not to say that Pinker necessarily is wrong to posit a substantial decline in homicide over time in Europe, or that he is mistaken to point to a "historical myopia" that leads us to magnify the scale of events near to us and to lose sight of the toll of conflicts before the twentieth century—"the closer an era is to our vantage point in the present, the more details we can make out"[34]—which many readily assume was "the bloodiest in history." He may well be right. Nevertheless, the use of quantitative evidence about "violence" or violent acts across the centuries to prove or disprove the point is fraught with diffi-culties, and consequently it may be better instead to examine what perhaps may be examined with greater certainty: changing and enhanced sensibili-ties toward violence. It is here, when he focuses on the "change in sensibil-ities," that Pinker is on firmer ground.

In the developed, Western world at least, public attitudes toward vio-lence have changed notably since the middle of the twentieth century. In the wake of World War I, the politics of violence and violent politics were accepted widely and even glorified. The 1914–1918 conflict had led to the destruction of communities, social structures, economic stability, and politi-cal frameworks. It not only precipitated revolution and revolutionary unrest but also eroded the normative constraints that had served increasingly to limit violence in public life during the nineteenth century. Welcoming the new world of violence precipitated by World War I, Ernst Jünger famously wrote: "This war is not the end but the beginning of violence. It is the forge in which the world will be hammered into new borders and new commu-nities. New forms want to be filled with blood, and power will be wielded with a hard fist. The war is a great school, and the new man will bear our stamp."[35]

We have come to regard the war as "the beginning of a *Zivilisationsbruch*, the rupture in civility that shook Europe to its foundations."[36] Both on the

Left and the Right of the political spectrum, violence often was regarded as the solution rather than the problem. In revolutionary Russia what distinguished the Bolsheviks from many of their competitors on the Left was their willingness to embrace extreme violence, from the Red Terror proclaimed in the summer of 1918, which resulted almost immediately in the shooting of hundreds of political prisoners in Petrograd, to the brutality with which the Civil War was fought, and to the deportation of almost a quarter of the entire Terek Cossak population in 1920.[37] The Bolsheviks, in the words of Laura Engelstein,

> torpedoed an established ethical system of norms—religion became a taboo, bourgeois legality despised, and standards of humanitarian (or, if one prefers, "chivalrous") conduct of warfare scorned. In their place emerged not a new form of social justice but rather the sanctioning (in the name of social justice) of forms of violent behavior: the taking of hostages, summary executions, looting, the murder of prisoners. All this became routine.[38]

On the other side of the political spectrum, both Italian fascism and German national socialism glorified violence and when in power made their violent ideologies real in campaigns of aggressive war and mass murder. Violence has long been regarded as "a fundamental ingredient," "the actual substance" of Italian fascism.[39] As Paul Corner has pointed out, "the politics of Fascism were always the politics of the bully; the Blackshirts never left anyone in doubt that violence against opponents was an acceptable method of action, a constituent part of Fascist 'style,' something frequently and proudly described as 'exquisitely Fascist.'"[40] German national socialism also glorified violence. Joseph Goebbels famously wrote in an account, first published in 1932 and reprinted many times subsequently, of the rise of the Nazi movement in Berlin, that the storm trooper "wants to fight, and he has a right to be led into battle. His existence only wins its justification by fighting."[41] But it was not just with the rise of the Hitler movement that violence became an accepted ingredient in German politics after World War I. Mark Jones has recently shown that the Weimar Republic was founded on violence, a process whereby "patterns of human behavior . . . allowed large sections of the German population to accept state-sponsored violence as a force for good."[42]

Politics conducted in a violent key found less resonance during the second half of the twentieth century. Public attitudes altered after World War II, which in this sense really was seen as the "war to end all wars."[43] The terrible shock of the extreme violence of and during World War II, often identified with the extremes of Auschwitz and Hiroshima, led many people to draw back, in what might be seen as a profound case of buyer's remorse. In states where political cultures had most embraced violence between the end of World War I and the aftermath of World War II, public attitudes subsequently changed remarkably. This change in attitudes after 1945 was particularly striking in Germany, where the aggressively violent and militaristic ideology of national socialism was succeeded during the second half of the twentieth century by an aversion to military service and a growing willingness to approve of conscientious objection.[44] A similar transformation occurred in postsurrender Japan, in which "the single most popular catch phrase . . . was *Heiwa Kokka Kensetsu*: 'Construct a Nation of Peace.'"[45] In both countries the shift in sensibilities was accompanied by a deep sense, in the immediate aftermath of the war, of having been the victims of violence—in particular of the Allied bombing campaigns—rather than its perpetrators.

The reactions against military conflict form but a part of the remarkable growth in sensitivity toward violence in Western societies in recent decades. Whether one focuses on the diminishing willingness to accept violence in politics, the widespread concern at the bombing of civilian targets, the growing awareness of domestic violence and the conviction that it is a matter of public concern and to be prosecuted, the ever-widening definition of PTSD, or the recent upsurge in concern about and condemnation of sexual harassment and abuse, sensitivity toward violence appears to have grown in recent decades, at least in the developed, Western world. Whatever the causes of this cultural shift—the shock of the eruptions of extreme violence during the first half of the twentieth century, the unprecedented economic boom that the West enjoyed after World War II that gave people more to lose through violence and less to gain, the increasing stability of state structures and their capability to maintain civil peace, the increased presence of women in the public sphere, the distancing of civil society in the West from war and the military, or the ways in which violence is reported in the media—it seems clear that sensibilities have changed.[46]

The change in sensibilities appears to offer the best support for Pinker's basic argument, in no case more clearly than with the heightened recognition of the serious nature of domestic and sexual violence. Domestic violence, sexual harassment, and rape within marriage are no longer tolerated to the extent that they were in the past; this unwillingness to ignore or accept such violence may suggest that indeed we have become less violent. But given what we know about violence, for example, in the United States, where in 2010 the National Intimate Partner and Sexual Violence Survey, which was based on over 16,000 interviews with both women and men, revealed that "nearly 1 in 5 women (18.3 percent) and 1 in 71 men (1.4 per cent) in the United States had been raped at some point in their lives,"[47] we should be careful about asserting that greater concern about violent acts necessarily means that fewer such acts in fact are being committed and that therefore "we have been getting kinder and gentler."

Conclusion

None of the processes sketched above necessarily is permanent or irreversible and in assessing them we need to be aware of short-term contingencies as well as of longer-term trends. Making his argument for a long-term decline in violence, Pinker refers repeatedly to Norbert Elias's influential analysis of the "process of civilization." However, Elias recognized that the civilization of which he wrote "is never completed and always endangered."[48] In this connection it is worth noting what Eric Monkonnen, a leading historian of violent crime, concluded in his last monograph, a perceptive quantitative study of murder in New York City: "We can learn something from the historical cycles in violence: as violent crime drifts downward now, we must be aware that in similar eras in the past, it always eventually turned upward again."[49] While Pinker is right to note the diminishing rates of violent crime reported in recent years, whether this and similar evidence actually establishes that as a species we really "have been getting kinder and gentler" is another matter. Perhaps it does; perhaps it does not. Whichever is the case, however, we should be grateful to Steven Pinker for placing the issue so forcefully into public debate.

Richard Bessel is Professor Emeritus of Twentieth-Century History at the University of York. He works on the social and political history of modern Germany, the aftermath of the two world wars, and the history of violence. His most recent books are Germany 1945: From War to Peace *(New York and London: Simon and Schuster, 2009),* Violence: A Modern Obsession *(New York and London: Simon and Schuster, 2015), and (edited, with Dorothee Wierling)* Inside World War One? The First World War and Its Witnesses *(Oxford: Oxford University Press, 2018).*

Notes

1. Steven Pinker, "A History of Violence," *The New Republic,* 19 March 2007, https://newrepublic.com/article/64340/history-violence-were-getting-nicer-every-day (accessed 13 March 2018).
2. Steven Pinker, *The Better Angels of Our Nature: The Decline of Violence in History and Its Causes* (London: Allen Lane, 2011), xxi.
3. Pinker, "A History of Violence."
4. Richard Bessel, *Violence: A Modern Obsession* (London: Simon & Schuster, 2015).
5. ". . . eine Wissenschaft, die Anworten auf die Fragen der Gegenwart gibt." Interview published 21 May 2013 on YouTube, https://youtu.be/s2J77x3mFUs (accessed 13 March 2018).
6. In this context it is worth noting that different groups in different societies have different propensities to report incidents of violent assault. See, for example, the interesting recent study by Janne Kivivuori, "Understanding Trends in Personal Violence: Does Cultural Sensitivity Matter?," *Crime and Justice* 43, no. 1 (2014): 322–324.
7. See Joanna Bourke, *Rape: A History from 1860 to the Present* (London: Virago Press, 2007), 307–328; Bessel, *Violence,* 175–183. It is worth noting in this context that among married women rape by husbands is many times more frequent than rape by strangers (Bourke, *Rape,* 320).

8. Pieter Spierenburg, "Faces of Violence: Homicide Trends and Cultural Meanings: Amsterdam, 1431–1816," *Journal of Social History* 27, no. 4 (1994): 710–716, here 701.

9. Pieter Spierenburg, interviewed by Professor Rod Broadhurst of the ANU College of Arts & Social Sciences, published in ANU TV on 22 October 2014, accessed on YouTube, https://www.youtube.com/watch?v=uOTdu4TfGFc (accessed 13 March 2018).

10. Pinker, *Better Angels,* 62.

11. Ibid., 61–62.

12. Ibid., 62–63.

13. Ibid., 116.

14. Howard Taylor, "Rationing Crime: The Political Economy of Criminal Statistics Since the 1850s," *The Economic History Review,* n.s., 51, no. 3 (1998): 569–590, here 569–570.

15. His Majesty's Stationery Office, *Census of England and Wales 1921: Preliminary Report* (London, 1921), 62, http://www.visionofbritain.org.uk/unit/10001043/cube/TOT_POP (accessed 13 March 2018).

16. Taylor, "Rationing Crime," 570–571.

17. Ibid., 588.

18. Spierenburg, "Faces of Violence," 706.

19. Roy Porter, *The Greatest Benefit to Mankind: A Medical History of Humanity from Antiquity to the Present* (London: HarperCollins, 1997), 615.

20. See Marie-Cécile Thoral, *From Valmy to Waterloo: France at War, 1792–1813* (London: Palgrave Macmillan, 2011), 80–81. Thoral notes, "Losses in the 2nd Battalion of the Ille-et-Vilaine in 1793 were 18.3 percent, but only 4 percent actually died in combat" (80). Most of the French casualties died in hospital.

21. François Vigo-Roussillon, *Journal de campagne, 1793–1837* (Paris: France-Empire, 1981), 51; quoted in Thoral, *From Valmy to Waterloo,* 81.

22. Porter, *The Greatest Benefit to Mankind,* 372.

23. Linda J. Bilmes, "Iraq's 100-Year Mortgage," *Foreign Policy,* no. 165 (March–April 2008): 84–85, here 84.

24. "The Blessings of Science on the Battlefield," *Scientific American* 109, no. 25 (20 December 1913): 477–481, here 477.

25. Anne Gulland, "Lessons from the Battlefield," *British Medical Journal* 336, no. 7653 (17 May 2008): 1098–1100, here 1098.

26. Figures from https://www.defense.gov/casualty.pdf (accessed 13 March 2018).

27. Using figures from Richard Bessel, *Germany after the First World War* (Oxford: Oxford University Press, 1993), 6.

28. Emily Buzzell and Samuel H. Preston, "Mortality of American Troops in the Iraq War," *Population and Development Review* 33, no. 3 (2007): 555–566, here 557.

29. See Ian Brown, "Logistics," in *The Cambridge History of the First World War,* vol. 2, *The State,* ed. Jay Winter (Cambridge: Cambridge University Press, 2014), 218–219.

30. Edgar Jones, "Historical Approaches to Post-Combat Disorders," *Philosophical Transactions: Biological Sciences* 361, no. 1468 (29 April 2006): 533–542, here 541. The study cited is E. Jones et al., "Post-Combat Syndromes from the Boer War to the Gulf: A Cluster Analysis of their Nature and Attribution," *British Medical Journal* 324, no. 7333 (2002): 321–324.

31. Robert J. Graham, "Vietnam: An Infantryman's View of Our Failure," *Military Affairs* 48, no. 3 (1984): 133–139, here 134.
32. Pinker, *Better Angels*, 60–64.
33. For example, the table on 195 of *Better Angels*.
34. Pinker, *Better Angels*, 193.
35. Ernst Jünger, *Der Kampf als Inneres Erlebnis* (Berlin: E. S.Mittler & Sohn, 1928), 70–71.
36. Michael Geyer, "War and the Context of General History in an Age of Total War: Comment on Peter Paret, 'Justifying the Obligation of Military Service,' and Michael Howard, 'World War One: The Crisis in European History,'" *Journal of Military History* 57, no. 5 (1993): 145–163, here 159–160.
37. The reference to the Petrograd shootings is in Adam Tooze, *The Deluge: The Great War and the Remaking of the Global Order, 1916–1931* (London: Allen Lane, 2014), 168. For discussion of the brutal violence of the Civil War, see especially Richard Pipes, *Russia under the Bolshevik Regime 1919–1924* (London: Fontana Press, 1995), 3–140; and Orlando Figes, *A People's Tragedy: The Russian Revolution 1891–1924* (London: Pimlico, 1997), 549–603. On the deportation of the Terek Cossaks, see Shane O' Rourke, "Trial Run: The Deportation of the Terek Cossaks 1920," in *Removing Peoples: Forced Removal in the Modern World*, ed. Richard Bessel and Claudia B. Haake (Oxford: Oxford University Press, 2009), 255–280.
38. Laura Engelstein, "Verhaltenswesen des Krieges in der Russischen Revolution: Zur moralischen Ökonomie der Gewalt," in *Zeitalter der Gewalt: Zur Geopolitik und Psychopolitik des Ersten Wetkriegs*, ed. Michael Geyer, Helmut Lethen, and Lutz Musner (Frankfurt am Main: Campus Verlag, 2015), 149–176, here 175.
39. Jens Petersen, "Violence in Italian Fascism, 1919–1925," in *Social Protest, Violence and Terror in Nineetenth- and Twentieth-Century Europe*, ed. Wolfgang J. Mommsen and Gerhard Hirschfeld (London: Macmillan, 1982), 275. Petersen quotes L. Salvatorelli and G. Mira, *Storia d'Italia nel periodo fascista* (Turin: Einaudi, 1957), 168.
40. Paul Corner, "Italian Fascism: Whatever Happened to Dictatorship?," *The Journal of Modern History* 74, no. 2 (2002): 325–351, here 331.
41. Joseph Goebbels, *Kampf um Berlin* (Munich: Eher, 1936), 30.
42. Mark Jones, *Founding Weimar: Violence and the German Revolution of 1918–1919* (Cambridge: Cambridge University Press, 2016), 3.
43. For this argument, see Richard Bessel, "The War to End All Wars: The Shock of Violence in 1945 and Its Aftermath in Germany," in *The No Man's Land of Violence: Extreme Wars in the 20th Century*, ed. Alf Lüdtke (Göttingen: Wallstein Verlag, 2006), 71–99.
44. Michael Geyer, "Cold War Angst: The Case of West-German Opposition to Rearmament and Nuclear Weapons," in *The Miracle Years: A Cultural History of West Germany, 1949–1968*, ed. Hanna Schissler (Princeton, NJ: Princeton University Press, 2001), 376–408; Richard Bessel, *Nazism and War* (New York: Random House, 2004), 199–201.
45. John W. Dower, *Embracing Defeat: Japan in the Wake of World War II* (New York: W. W. Norton, 1999), 176.
46. This argument is developed in detail in Bessel, *Violence*.
47. Michele C. Black, Kathleen C. Basile, Matthew J. Breiding, Sharon G. Smith, Mikel L. Walters, Melissa T. Merrick, Jieru Chen, and Mark R. Stevens, "National Intimate Partner and Sexual Violence Survey: 2010 Summary Report" (Atlanta,

2011), 1–2, https://www.cdc.gov/violenceprevention/pdf/nisvs_report2010-a .pdf (accessed 13 March 2018).
48. Norbert Elias, "Zivilisation und Gewalt: Über das Staatsmonopol der körperlichen Gewalt und seine Durchbrechungen," in *Studien über die Deutschen: Machtkämpfe und Habitusentwicklung im 19. und 20. Jahrhundert* (Frankfurt am Main: Suhrkamp, 1994), 225.
49. Eric H. Monkonnen, *Murder in New York City* (London: University of California Press, 2001), 181.

Chapter 7

The "Moral Effect" of Legalized Lawlessness

Violence in Britain's Twentieth-Century Empire

Caroline Elkins

By the summer of 1938, the Arab Revolt in Mandatory Palestine had been raging for some two years and Britain had lost control of the situation. All sides of the imperial divide terrorized Arab villagers, and the rebels dominated the countryside, where they destroyed vast swaths of Palestine's infrastructure. As Britain scrambled to reassemble a new leadership cadre to take charge and crush the rebellion once and for all, a lone intelligence officer, Captain Orde Wingate, stepped forward with an idea to "terrorize the terrorists . . . [to] catch them and just wipe them out."[1] Officials at the highest level endorsed Wingate's brainchild—the Special Night Squads—and, with it, the plan "to set up a system and undetected movement of troops and police by night, across country and into villages, surprising gangs, restoring confidence to peasants, and gaining government control of rural areas." For Wingate and his superior officers, translating Britain's superior "national character" and prowess in training and natural aggression into a highly disciplined counterterror operation with the single goal of wiping out Arab rebels was the key to reestablishing British colonial control.[2]

Wingate's Third Force took its brand of counterterrorism straight to the heart of the Arab villages. The Special Night Squads soon earned their legendary status when body counts and repression were the barometers for success. On their captain's orders, Wingate's men preferred inflicting bodily harm with blood-staining and dismembering bayonets and bombs rather than bullets; their leader's "morality of punishment" also inspired them.[3] Reprisals became part of the squads' repertoire, with oil-soaked sand stuffed into the mouths of uncooperative Arabs. Wingate boasted how "anyone hanging about the line for an unlawful purpose was liable swiftly and silently to vanish away."[4]

Britain's empire would become as renowned for creating civil wars as they would be for leaving them in its wake, and Palestine was no exception. The Special Night Squads would become a training ground for future Jewish insurgents, both against Britain and eventually the Arab population. So, too, did the squads embrace a wide swath of British security forces, some of whom, like Corporal Fred Howbrook and Lieutenant Rex King-Clark, were professional soldiers trained to kill.[5] Others, when the Special Night Squads expanded, were like the inexperienced, job-seeking Sydney Burr, who, on a policing contract in Palestine, only knew Arabs as "wogs" and casually recounted at the time how "most of the information we get is extracted by third degree methods, it is the only way with these people."[6] Many of these men were young, rough-and-ready recruits who were steeped in the Black and Tan traditions that suffused the Palestine Police Force after many within the Irish forces took up posts in the Mandate after 1922.

From the start, Arab politicians, including president of the Palestine Arab Delegation to the League of Nations Jamal al-Husayni, as well as European missionaries, local colonial officials, residents of Palestine, and military and police personnel, documented Britain's repressive measures targeted primarily at the Palestinian Arab population—measures that were embraced not only by Special Night Squads, but also at every level of British military, policing, and colonial administrations.[7] Accounts of torture and humiliation, murder, and systemized suffering were privately brought to Britain's successive high commissioners in Palestine, as well as to the archbishop of the Anglican Church and Britain's War and Colonial Offices.[8] A common refrain emerged as official responses rebounded in liberalism's echo chamber of denials—denials well rehearsed in previous imperial dramas. In this instance, such lies and exaggerations, according to myriad British officials, were the handiwork of Arab propagandists, fueled in no small way by the opportunistic inveigling of Europe's rising fascist tide that sought to discredit the good name of Britain and its empire.[9] Prime Minister Neville Chamberlain's cabinet went so far as to dismiss the flow of allegations from Palestine as "absolutely baseless," and declared "the character of the British soldier is too well known to require vindication."[10]

Still, al-Husayni persisted and appealed to the League of Nations. Gesturing to the situation's gravity through historical analogy, he wrote: "Such atrocities of the dark ages, to which the human race, nowadays, look back with disgust and horror, of torturing men during criminal investigation and assaulting peaceful people and destroying their properties wholesale when peacefully lying within their homes are actions that have daily been perpetrated in the Holy Land during the greater part of the last three years."

The letter's analogous flair then gave way to specificity. Among other excesses, al-Husayni described the "scorching" of body parts with "hot iron rods," "severe beating with lashes," the "pulling out [of] nails and scorching the skin under them by special appliances," and the "pulling of the sexual organs." He detailed the British forces' widespread ransacking and looting of homes, summary executions, disappearances, the denial of food and water to innocent civilians, the rape of women and girls, and the destruction of livestock. The diplomat then closed his appeal, reminding the league that "if the Mandatory [power of Britain] is innocent of these excesses then our demand for a neutral enquiry should be welcomed by all concerned."[11]

While the outcome of al-Husayni's appeal hung in an international balance weighted by the realpolitik of fascism's advances, so too was it calibrated within liberalism's framework of permissible norms. These norms did not spring from Europe's pressing exigencies of the late 1930s, but rather were deeply rooted in the *longue durée* of liberal imperialism's spread, particularly in Britain and its empire. There, stretching back before the Victorian era, conceptions of brown and black subjects, the justifications for—if not the necessity of—violence, and moral claims to a superior civilization created a tapestry of ideas that found expression in colonial administrations, imperial security forces, enabling legal scaffoldings, policies of divide and rule, and nationalist conceptions of Britain and the benevolent myths that belied them. So too did they find expression in the League of Nations' Permanent Mandates Commission, which was as much a reflection of liberal imperialism's agenda as it was an oversight agent for its alleged transgressions.

The degree to which al-Husayni was aware of the mutually informing ideological, political, and structural forces working against him is uncertain. Even so, this skilled and measured diplomat surely had some inclination of the ways in which interwar Palestine was a cauldron of ideas, institutions, and personalities that had been incubated elsewhere in the imperial world. This world was one in which violence, even in its most severe forms, had evolved into a framework that was not simply justificatory but was also internalized by many of those wielding power, from the highest reaches of decision making to the lowest levels of execution, as de rigueur.

By the eve of World War II, it was in Mandatory Palestine where decades of liberal imperialist ideas and practices that had matured across the British Empire would descend and consolidate in the most dramatic and consequential of ways. The reach and impact of these ideas and practices, as well as the individuals executing them, would extend well beyond al-Husayni's Palestine and the league's pending response to the repressive watermarks staining the Mandate's files to a post–World War II future where Britain would systematically deploy violence—normalized over decades, if not centuries—in its last gasp effort to hang onto empire and secure a place in the New World Order.

In the case of Palestine, and indeed much of the twentieth-century Anglo-colonial world, British liberalism gave rise to a framework of permissible norms and logics of violence in empire that myriad scholars often misunderstand, if they examine it at all. When Steven Pinker suggests that violence was on the decline and humanitarianism on the rise in the twentieth century, he offers the myth of British imperial benevolence an academic fillip that can scarcely withstand empirical scrutiny. Pinker ignores copious amounts of historical evidence, including countless files documenting Britain's creation and deployment of violent repression in 1930s Palestine and elsewhere in the empire, not to mention the lived experiences of hundreds of millions of black and brown people, some of whom offer detailed accounts of systematic violence throughout the twentieth-century British imperial world, through memoirs, appeals to British and international commissions, letters to Colonial Office, newspaper articles, and other sources.

Had Pinker interrogated violence in the British Empire fully and, with it, my 2005 publication *Imperial Reckoning: The Untold Story of Britain's Gulag in Kenya,* he would have been aware of the systemized violence that Britain deployed during the Mau Mau Emergency in colonial Kenya.[12] He might also, at a minimum, have gestured to the connections between 1950s Kenya and other theaters of British imperial violence, such as those in Palestine, both before and after World War II. Had he widened his aperture, he might have located the genesis of twentieth-century British colonial violence in two processes: the birth of liberal imperialism and the evolution of legalized lawlessness in the empire. Together, they provided the ideological and legal apparatuses necessary for Britain's repeated deployment of systematized violence in far-flung corners of the globe.

Liberal imperialism, the twinned birthing of liberalism and imperialism in the nineteenth century, gave rise to liberal authoritarianism. This ideology, which underpinned Britain's civilizing mission, took form in various enabling legal scaffoldings, including the evolution of martial law into emergency regulations, or statutory martial law, as well as the parallel consolidation of military doctrine and law around the issues of force. These reinforcing processes unfolded from the turn of the nineteenth century and continued through the interwar period and into the era of decolonization after World War II. On the ground, various forms of systemized violence evolved in Sudan and the South African War, then the Easter Rising in Ireland, Amritsar, the evolution of air control in Iraq, the Egyptian uprising, the Irish War of Independence, the ongoing acts of revolutionary violence in Bengal, Western Wall violence, and the Arab Revolt, where their coalescence and maturity created particular, British imperial-inspired forms of legalized lawlessness. Once crystalized, it is hardly surprising that these same policies and practices—often transferred from one hot spot to the next by shared cadres of colonial and military officers and footmen—unfolded in the late 1940s and 1950s on massive scales in colonies like Malaya, Kenya, and Cyprus. There, detention without trial, torture, forced labor, and starvation became routine tactics in suppressing so-called terrorists demanding their independence from British colonial rule.

Locating the ideological framework for systematized violence in the British Empire takes us back to the nineteenth century. The extension of Britain's global power and domination brought with it history-defining debates about universal principles, free markets, the protection of property, and rule of law, and importantly, who was and was not entitled to the rights and responsibilities of citizenship. As liberal thought evolved in Europe, it intersected with the rise of empires. There was a mutually constitutive relationship between liberalism and imperialism that would have profound consequences on British conceptions of liberty, progress, and governance both at home and abroad.[13]

Defining much of British thought was the categorical assumption that a parochial Western liberalism, intrinsically universal, belonged to all people worldwide. Yet, there were deep contradictions in the liberal imperial project, ones that were increasingly understood through a racial lens. John Stuart Mill juxtaposed civilization and barbarism to create new ideological idioms. He advocated for a progressive notion of citizenship and a narrative of human development that was intimately bound with Britain's civilizing mission.[14] Good government in empire had to be adjusted to local "stages of civilization," with John Stuart Mill advocating for a paternalistic form of despotism to tutor empire's children. According to Mill, "a civilized government, to be really advantageous to [subject populations], will require to be in a considerable degree despotic: one over which they do not themselves exercise control, and which imposes a great amount of forcible restraint upon their actions."[15] In effect, England had a right, if not a responsibility, to rule despotically to reform the barbarous populations of the world.

Universalist ideas gave way to culture and history conditioning human character. In an emerging global citizenry, inclusivity would come in stages, if ever. With Britain's political ascendancy over subject populations, Mill declared that "the same rules of international morality do not apply between civilized nations and between civilized nations and barbarians."[16] Although written in the mid-Victorian era, echoes of Mill's exclusion of "barbarians" from the "international morality" of the "civilized nations" would resonate in twentieth-century justifications and denials of repression, as well as the denial of human rights laws to imperial subjects.[17] As empire expanded, and subject populations refused to conform to British conceptions of progress and civilizing largesse, Mill's liberal imperialism, which denied individual sovereignty to brown and black peoples around the world, while holding out the promise of reform, opened the justificatory door to coercion as an instrument of colonial rule.[18]

A series of violent events in empire would harden notions of imperial subjects and their rights. The heroic civilizing mission, despite a rhetorical staying power that Pinker's work so ably embraces, would, in practice, be greatly eviscerated and replaced with a moral disillusionment and disavowal of liberalism's capacity to transform the backward peoples of empire, at least in part. In its place would enter a British imperial rule that, while still projecting its moral claims of the civilizing mission, accentuated and codified difference, and countenanced the threat and deployment of various forms of violence. The Indian Rebellion of 1857, followed by the Morant Bay Rebellion in Jamaica and with it the Governor Eyre crisis, would precipitate this volte-face. The Anglo-imperial pendulum swung in the conservative direction, with the likes of Thomas Carlyle and James Fitzjames Stephen leveraging the moment to further authoritarian views on imperial rule. They castigated Mill's "sentimental liberalism," which reputedly undermined political stability in the empire and at home. For his part, Stephen was relentless, asserting an unapologetic racial superiority and advocating for absolute rule in the colonies and, with it, the necessity of coercion. As far as Mill's beloved rule of law was concerned—a rule of law important to Pinker's thesis—Stephen did not hedge, writing, "Force is an absolutely essential element of all law whatever. Indeed law is nothing but regulated force subjected to particular conditions and directed toward particular objects."[19]

In retrospect, the liberal in Britain's liberal authoritarianism is often difficult to discern in empire. Initial acts of conquest would give way in the twentieth century to elaborate legal codes, the proliferation of police and security forces, circumscriptions on free market economies for the colonized, and administrative apparatuses that marginalized and oppressed entire populations while fueling racial and ethnic divisions within and between them. The lived realities of Britain's burden in the empire would be vastly different from the nation's self-representations, grounded as they were in an historical consciousness that was equally as deft at collective erasure and creating approbatory versions of the nation's past as it was in disseminating these ideas through liberalism's official and unofficial channels.

Had Pinker acknowledged liberalism's obfuscating abilities, he would have discovered the paradox between lived, imperial experiences of the colonized and the laudatory claims of Britain's civilizing mission. Indeed, the power of liberalism's obfuscations can be traced not only in the persistence of British imperial myths in today's Anglo-popular culture, but also in scholarly works such as Pinker's that fail to interrogate the erasures and denials—like those put forth during the Arab Revolt—that litter Britain's colonial past. Nor do these works unpack the mutual constitution of liberalism and imperialism and, with it, a dominant narrative of universal human emancipation, equality, rights, and the civilizing mission that materialized simultaneously with an underbelly of repression as expressed in evolutionary thought, racism, class, and sexism. The privileged media through which liberalism would do its work, including bureaucracy, mass media, law, literacy, and the scholarly academy, became the means of emancipation and inclusion, as well as the tools of repression and obfuscation.

The evolution of legalized lawlessness and its coexistence with an evolv-ing military doctrine was, in many ways, an epiphenomenon of liberal au-thoritarianism. Racial and cultural difference became institutionalized at every level of executive, legislative, and judicial rule in the British Empire. That military doctrine also reflected the "rule of colonial difference" pervad-ing British discourse, practices, and institutions at home and in the empire should scarcely be surprising.[20] As Britain kept ticking off imperial, small wars and other eruptions of violence, its military increasingly considered best practices for dealing with so-called recalcitrant natives—or terrorists, as was often the term. In turn, these practices would become part of the broader institutionalization of violence; these were best captured in the work of Colonel Charles Callwell, a major figure in the study of counterinsur-gency practices throughout the twentieth century. His *Small Wars: Their Prin-ciples and Practices,* originally written in 1896, and updated after he served as a staff officer and commander in the South African War, would become the starting point for nearly all counterinsurgency theorists and practitioners, even to the present day.[21] Callwell's expansive work synthesized not only Britain's military engagements throughout the empire, but also drew lessons from French, Spanish, American, and Russian campaigns, among others. Together, these reference points would provide him with a range of histori-cal examples that supported not only the perceived short-term effectiveness of unbridled force, but also an ideological framework that understood such repressive measures to be a reflection of liberalism's underbelly.

For Callwell, when European troops were engaged in wars against the "uncivilized" and "savage" populations of the world, as opposed to civilized armies, a different set of rules were needed.[22] Callwell pointed to the "moral force of civilization" underwriting European superiority, and the need to teach "savage" peoples "a lesson which they will not forget."[23] It was not only the strategic advantage of such measures that Callwell endorsed in waging total destruction against the enemy. Rather, he emphasized in his treatise the "moral effect" that brutality wrought upon "uncivilized" pop-ulations, writing: "[The] object is not only to prove to the opposing force unmistakably which is the stronger, but also to inflict punishment on those who have taken up arms . . . [The] enemy must be made to feel a moral in-feriority throughout . . . [Fanatics and savages] must be thoroughly brought to book and cowed or they will rise again."[24]

Callwell's "moral effect" reflected the military's ease of fusing the "white man's burden" with battlefield strategies to produce a morality of violence that belied imperial confrontations around the globe. At once racist and perversely paternalistic, Callwell's moralistic terms nonetheless suggest the ways in which British military doctrine reproduced the Victorian-era norms of liberal imperialism, norms that understood the uses of violent measures to be a necessary part of ensuring order and civilizing the backward races of the world.[25] With its binaries of good versus evil framing justifications of violence in the empire, liberal imperialism was not simply an exculpatory ideology. It both shaped and reflected self and national understandings in parliamentary debates, media outlets, popular culture, and commemorative acts. It also shaped military thinking and practices for Callwell and many of his successors in future colonial conflicts, from the highest-ranking officials to the ordinary soldier.[26] In the years ahead, the main issue would be the legal and political frameworks necessary to accommodate Callwell's punitive violence. Once conventional warfare methods were jettisoned, "it is then that the regular troops," according to Callwell, "are forced to resort to cattle lifting and village burning and that the war assumes an aspect which may shock the humanitarian."[27]

Turning historically to empire, there was a parallel evolution of legal and political norms that reflected Britain's on-the-ground deployment of violence, as articulated in Callwell's treatise. Whereas government by consent increasingly defined England, Scotland, and Wales in the nineteenth century, order was imposed upon Ireland, for example, through a series of Insurrection Acts, Habeas Corpus Suspension Acts, and deployments of martial law. When these were not sufficient, Coercion Acts were introduced, with measures to control arms, provide for special systems of trial, and criminalize oath taking. At the time, the jurist and constitutionalist theorist Albert Dicey made clear that the Coercion Acts were fully incompatible with the rule of law and the ideals of civil liberties, stating that "in principle . . . thoroughly vicious . . . [it] in effect gave the Irish executive an unlimited power of arrest; it established in them a despotic government . . . [It] could not be made permanent, and applied to the whole United Kingdom without depriving every citizen of security for his person freedom."[28] Ultimately, the acts became the precursors for modern states of emergency whose legal codes transferred repressive powers to civilian authorities who, in turn, could declare a state of emergency, or the English equivalent of a state of siege. This was distinct from the declaration of martial law, and significantly for Ireland and other parts of the empire, little under the Coercion Acts conferring emergency-like powers could be questioned in a court of law.[29]

Looking elsewhere in the empire, the Defence of India Act was passed in 1915, and was sweeping in its repressive scope. The act enabled India's executive to pass any regulation to secure the public safety and defense of the British Raj. In Bengal alone, some eight hundred orders were put into force, eviscerating civil and political liberties, such as existed.[30] When Britain turned to arming the civilian state in Ireland with the Easter Rising in 1916, and later what became the Irish War of Independence, they did so through a host of highly authoritarian acts. Wielding a legally enabled strategy of coercion, Whitehall and its Dublin Castle counterpart fueled a war that quickly descended into an intensified bloodbath of killings, reprisals, and counterreprisals. It was also a conflict that witnessed a deployment of both military and police forces—including the notorious Black and Tans and Auxiliaries—who helped carry out legalized reprisals in the final months of the Irish War of Independence, along with a host of other repressive measures, before many of their members moved on to Palestine at the war's end.

Indeed, returning to the Mandate in the 1930s, the British government undertook a series of steps that consolidated decades of legalized lawlessness into a set of emergency powers that would become the most popular model for future counterinsurgency campaigns. In 1931, the Palestine (Defence) Order in Council was passed; this conferred upon the high commissioner a set of powers that exceeded any similar legislation to date. Based upon earlier codes in Ireland and India, and stretching back to the Irish Act of 1833, the Order in Council empowered the high commissioner to declare a state of emergency, and thereby issue and amend regulations for arrest, detention without trial, censorship, deportation, and trial by military courts. With the 1936 Arab general strike, the high commissioner declared a state of emergency in Palestine and issued the first of a series of regulations and amending orders that included the power to demolish buildings, including villages and homes, and the imposition of the death penalty for discharging firearms and sabotaging phone and rail lines.[31]

Still, the military wanted more legal coverage to unleash an all-out assault on the Arab population. The top brass believed the emergency regulations were inadequate, particularly in light of the punitive destruction of property and the unleashing of reprisals that had been permissible in Ireland. After some hand-wringing by the Colonial Office's legal minds in London, it was determined that martial law would, in fact, be too restrictive on the military and the punitive actions of its soldiers, as the civil courts were still sitting in Palestine and they might challenge repressive military actions. In martial law's place came the Palestine Martial Law (Defence) Order in Council of 26 September 1936, and subsequently a new Palestine (Defence) Order in Council on 18 March 1937. With it, Section 6 (1) stated the high commissioner "may make such Regulations . . . as appear to him in his unfettered discretion to be necessary or expedient for securing the public safety, the defence of Palestine, the maintenance of public order and the suppression of mutiny, rebellion and riot, and for maintaining supplies and services essential to the life of the community."[32]

Shades of empire's Victorian-era past were cast into the Mandate's present when Stephen's nineteenth-century avowal that "law is nothing but regulated force" was taken to its logical, liberal authoritarian conclusion in Palestine. There, the high commissioner, and with him, all security forces—including the police and military—could do whatever they liked, which included all measures already on the books, as well as punitive destruction of property, trial by military courts without right to appeal, and the sweeping away of any form of judicial review. Statutory martial law was now in effect, and when put into practice, army command—under the auspices of the high commissioner—would have the upper hand.[33] The legalization of lawlessness, ideologically rooted in the birthing of liberal imperialism, and evolving over decades in various theaters of empire, was now fully matured.[34]

Operating in parallel with Britain's Colonial Office, the War Office ensured its field officers and soldiers a wide berth in defining and implementing the use of force. In 1929, the military manual was revised to take the events in Amritsar into account, though in practice little changed. The manual made clear that "the existence of an armed insurrection would justify the use of any degree of force necessary effectually to meet and cope with the insurrection" and loosely defined "collective punishments," "reprisals," and "retributions," all of which could "inflict suffering upon innocent individuals . . . [and were] indispensible as a last resort."[35] Between the military's own code of conduct and the civil emergency measures that offered legal coverage, Britain's troops, along with the local police force, operated virtually without restraint or fear of prosecution. When the steady stream of complaints and accounts of atrocities in late 1930s Palestine piled up on the desks of Palestine's chief secretary and on those of officials back in London's Colonial and War Offices (where they would later similarly amass during the end of empire wars that shaped and defined the British Empire in the 1950s), almost nothing, legally, needed to be done. In the few cases where prosecutions took place, acquittals were more the norm than the exception.

In the end, the Permanent Mandates Commission never investigated British actions in Palestine. Jamal al-Husanyi's letter remained in the League of Nations' inbox, unanswered. World War II intervened before the commission could respond, though chances are, as it had with multiple other complaints detailing British colonial violence in Palestine, the commission would have dismissed al-Husanyi's as well. In fact, in an era of imperial internationalism, some might conclude that the Permanent Mandates Commission was part of the problem, at least in Palestine, where it had chastised the British for not having been coercive enough in crushing the rebellion.[36] In effect, the presumed oversight committee endorsed, with a similar moralizing refrain that echoed the likes of Wingate, Callwell, and others, the use of violence against colonial subjects.

Still, al-Husanyi's letter was scarcely written in vain. It offers one footprint, along with thousands of others that litter the archives, of Britain's deployment of systematic violence in its twentieth-century empire. And, while al-Husanyi and Arab Palestinians never received a proper hearing of their complaints, other imperial subjects eventually would. In 2009, the British Empire was put on trial for the first time when, in London's High Court of Justice, five elderly Kikuyu claimants charged the British government with overseeing a system of torture and violence in the detention camps of late colonial Kenya. *Imperial Reckoning* was the historical basis for the case, and I was expert witness for the claimants. At the time of the filing, the Foreign and Commonwealth Office—the named defendant in the case—vehemently denied any misdeeds in its former empire, much like the Chamberlain government in Palestine's yesteryear, and vowed to fight the case to the bitter end.

Pinker was surely aware of the historic Mau Mau case, as it was splashed across major newspapers in Britain. Yet, much like Foreign Secretary William Hague, he chose to dismiss the piles of evidence that tell a damning story of systematic violence in colonial Kenya—violence that was scarcely an anomaly to Britain's East African colony. Ultimately, however, after a four-year legal battle, the British government changed course, and in June 2013, Foreign Secretary Hague rose in the House of Commons and offered Britain's first-ever acknowledgment, and apology for, its use of systematic violence in empire, and with it, a £20 million payment to over five thousand Kikuyu victims of British torture in the detention camps of Kenya. In effect, the British government could no longer hide behind liberalism's obfuscations and moral claims that denied the imbrication of violence in its civilizing mission. The evidence—much of which was available to Pinker during his research—was simply too overwhelming. The evidence from myriad other former British colonies, such as al-Husanyi's Palestine, were also available to Pinker, yet he chose to ignore it, or perhaps deny its validity. Yet, it is this very denial of evidence, particularly from hundreds of millions of former brown and black colonial subjects, that render works like Pinker's so damaging in the postcolonial present. Denied their lived experiences, these men and women are nonetheless etched in memories throughout the world. These collective memories scarcely need historians armed with archival data to help them jettison Pinker's Western-centric claims that violence declined in colonial landscapes during twentieth-century British rule.

Caroline Elkins is Professor of History and of African and African American Studies at Harvard University, and Visiting Professor of Business Administration at Harvard Business School. Her first book, Imperial Reckoning: The Untold Story of Britain's Gulag in Kenya, *won the Pulitzer Prize for General Nonfiction and was the basis for the historic Mau Mau case in Britain's High Court of Justice. Knopf will publish her next book on British colonial violence in the twentieth century in 2019.*

Notes

1. Imperial War Museum (IWM), Sound Archive, Accession 4619, Fred Howbrook.
2. IWM, Document Collection, 4623, Private Papers of Major General H.E.N. Bredin, "Appreciation by Captain OC Wingate, of Force HQ Intelligence on 5.6.38 at NAZARETH of the possibilities of night movements by armed forces of the Crown with the object of putting an end to terrorism in Northern Palestine."
3. John Bierman and Colin Smith, *Fire in the Night: Wingate of Burma, Ethiopia, and Zion* (New York: Random House, 1999), 115.
4. Bierman and Smith, *Fire in the Night,* 115–116; Liddell Hart Centre for Military Archives (LHCMA), King's College London, United Kingdom, Captain B.H. Liddell Hart Papers, GB0099, 11/1936-1938, Captain O.C. Wingate OCSNS, "Report of Operations carried out by Special Night Squads on Night of 11/12 July 1938."
5. R. King-Clark, *Free for a Blast* (London: Grenville Publishing Company Limited, 1988), 157.

6. IWM, Department of Documents, 88/8/1, Private Papers of S. Burr, Letter c. June 1937; for use of the term "wogs" see multiple letters in the file, including July 9, 1937; December 20, 1937; c. March 1938; and c. April 1938.
7. For example, see Middle East Centre Archive (MECA), St. Antony's College, Oxford, United Kingdom, GB165-0161, Jerusalem and East Mission, Boxes 61 and 66.
8. Ibid.
9. For example, Hansard, *House of Commons Debate (HCD)*, vol. 341, cc 1988, November 24, 1938.
10. TNA, WO 32/4562, Memorandum from G.D. Roseway to C.G.L. Syers, January 12, 1939.
11. TNA, WO/32/4562, Letter from Jamaal Husseini, President, Palestine Arab Delegation, to His Excellency, The President of the Permanent Mandates Commission, June 12, 1939.
12. Caroline Elkins, *Imperial Reckoning: The Untold Story of Britain's Gulag in Kenya* (New York: Henry Holt, 2005).
13. The subsequent analysis draws upon a range of works, including Thomas R. Metcalf, *Ideologies of the Raj* (Cambridge: Cambridge University Press, 1994); Uday Singh Mehta, *Liberalism and Empire: A Study in Nineteenth-Century British Liberal Thought* (Chicago: Chicago University Press, 1999); Karuna Mantena, *Alibis of Empire: Henry Maine and the Ends of Liberal Imperialism* (Princeton, NJ: Princeton University Press, 2010); and Jennifer Pitts, *A Turn to Empire: The Rise of Imperial Liberalism in Britain and France* (Princeton, NJ: Princeton University Press, 2005.
14. See, for example, Eileen P. Sullivan, "Liberalism and Imperialism: J. S. Mill's Defense of the British Empire," *Journal of the History of Ideas* 44, no. 4 (1983): 599–617.
15. John Stuart Mill, *Considerations on Representative Government* (New York: CreateSpace, 2014), 4. Originally published 1861.
16. As quoted in Sullivan, "Liberalism and Imperialism," 610.
17. Mantena makes a similar point in *Alibis of Empire,* 33.
18. See, for example, Nadia Urbinati, "The Many Heads of the Hydra: J. S. Mill on Despotism," in *J. S. Mill's Political Thought: A Bicentennial Reassessment,* ed. Nadia Urbinati and Alex Zakaras (Cambridge: Cambridge University Press, 2007), 66–97, here 74–75.
19. James Fitzjames Stephen, *Liberty, Equality, Fraternity,* ed. Stuart D. Warner (Indianapolis, IN: Liberty Fund, 1993), 111.
20. Partha Chatterjee, *The Nation and Its Fragments* (Princeton, NJ: Princeton University Press, 1993), 10.
21. Colonel C. E. Callwell, *Small Wars: Their Principles and Practices* (Lincoln: University of Nebraska Press, 1996).
22. The terms "uncivilized" and "savage" are deployed throughout Callwell's writings.
23. Callwell, *Small Wars,* 102.
24. Ibid., 41, 72, 148.
25. Ian F. W. Becket suggests a similar point in *Modern Insurgencies and Counter-Insurgencies: Guerrillas and their Opponents since 1750* (London: Routledge, 2001), 25, 183.

26. Daniel Whittingham, "'Savage Warfare': C. E. Callwell, the Roots of Counter-insurgency, and the Nineteenth-Century Context," in *British Ways of Counter-insurgency: A Historical Perspective*, ed. Matthew Hughes (London: Routledge, 2013), 13–29, here 14.

27. Callwell, *Small Wars*, 40.

28. A. V. Dicey, *The Case against Home Rule* (London: John Murray, 1886), 117.

29. A. W. Brian Simpson, *Human Rights and the End of Empire: Britain and the Genesis of the European Convention* (Oxford: Oxford University Press, 2011), 78–80; and Gerard Hogan and Clive Walker, *Political Violence: Political Violence and the Law in Ireland* (Manchester: Manchester University Press, 1989), 12–14.

30. Simpson, *Human Rights*, 82.

31. Ibid., 84–85.

32. Ibid., 86.

33. Matthew Hughes, "The Banality of Brutality: British Armed Forces and the Repression of the Arab Revolt in Palestine, 1936–1939," *The English Historical Review* 124, no. 507 (April 2009): 313–334, here 318.

34. Simpson, *Human Rights*, 85–86.

35. *Manual of Military Law* (London: HMSO, 1929), 103, 255; and Hughes, "Banality of Brutality," 316–317.

36. For a discussion of the League of Nations as "an eminently Victorian institution," see Mark Mazower, *No Enchanted Palace: The End of Empire and the Ideological Origins of the United Nations* (Princeton, NJ: Princeton University Press, 2009), 21.

Chapter 8

Does *Better Angels of Our Nature* Hold Up as History?

Randolph Roth

My late friend and colleague at Ohio State, historian Joseph Lynch, said many memorable things. But one of my favorites was: "Every time I read a great book, a little piece of me dies." It is hard not to envy Steven Pinker's *Better Angels of Our Nature*. It is a great book, one which I think most every historian of violence wishes she or he could have written, whether they agree with its argument or not. Its writing is graceful; its insights are keen; and the author's knowledge, which ranges from the humanities to the sciences and social sciences, is both deep and broad. It is a tour de force. Together with Pieter Spierenburg's *A History of Murder, Better Angels* is a comprehensive and compelling defense of Norbert Elias's "civilization thesis": the idea that historical forces have led over millennia to a long-term decline in all forms of violence in human societies, lethal and nonlethal.[1]

Elias was not naïve. He realized, writing in the 1930s, that Europe was far from a peaceful place and that many Europeans were still inclined to violence. But he believed that modern Europeans were fundamentally different from medieval Europeans. Elias, who was influenced deeply by Sigmund Freud's theory of the subconscious, believed that humans are by nature creatures of instinct, driven by irrational psychological forces that could be contained but never eliminated by the forces of civilization (represented first by our parents and then by society at large). He believed that medieval Europeans were more murderous because they were less repressed, or less "civilized," than contemporary Europeans: more spontaneous, more emotional, and thus less capable of controlling their base impulses when they faced a challenge or had an opportunity to dominate, exploit, or humiliate another human being. Over time, the forces of "civilization" gained the upper hand and reshaped the psyche of modern Europeans, rendering them more capable of censoring their behavior and controlling their base impulses, and thus less prone to violence.

Pinker, a distinguished psychologist, rejects Elias's Freudianism in favor of a contemporary theory of the human psyche, rooted in evolutionary theory. In Pinker's view, evolution has given humans capacities for cooperative and aggressive behavior. History has not, in his opinion, been shaped by a struggle between the id and the superego, but by a struggle between the "better angels" of human nature (empathy, self-control, moral sense, and reason) and humanity's "inner demons" (predation, dominance, revenge, sadism, and ideology).[2] Pinker agrees, however, with Elias that historical circumstances have tended more and more over time to deter aggression in human societies and to facilitate cooperation and forbearance. He does not argue that the world today is nonviolent, or that it ever will be. But he believes human societies have become less violent over time, despite periodic reversals, and that they are less violent today than ever before.

Pinker contends, in line with other "civilization" theorists, that there are five basic reasons for the long-term decline in violence:

1. Leviathan: We have created strong states with monopolies on the legitimate use of force, which can suppress feuding, raiding, and vigilantism.

2. Commerce: People have reason to prefer the mutually advantageous exchange of goods, services, and ideas to expropriation, exploitation, and extermination.

3. Feminization: By empowering women, states have undermined the glorification of violence and the dangerous, exclusively male subcultures that have been responsible for most violence.

4. Cosmopolitanism: Literacy, mobility, and mass media have advanced to the point where they "can prompt people to take the perspective of people unlike themselves and to expand their circle of sympathy to embrace them."

5. The escalator of reason: "The application of knowledge and rationality to human affairs" has led people to "recognize the futility of cycles of violence" and to "reframe violence as a problem to be solved rather than a contest to be won."

These forces have gained strength globally, according to Pinker, since the rise of the first great agrarian states in ancient times. Their progress has been slow and uneven, but nonetheless remarkable, and more rapid since the

Enlightenment, a movement that represents in Pinker's opinion what humanity can achieve at its best.[3]

The "civilization thesis" has been embraced by many historians of violence since Elias first articulated it in the 1930s. But Pinker has made a valuable contribution by synthesizing a wider range of evidence in support of the thesis than anyone before, and by grounding the thesis in a more robust theory of human psychology.

Nonetheless, I think Pinker's theory, like previous versions of the civilization thesis, is wrong. It does not hold up as history, for three basic reasons. First, the evidence gathered to date by historians does not show a long-term decline in interpersonal or collective violence since the medieval era. Second, the historical forces that Pinker sees as deterrents to violence are in fact, like most historical forces, Janus-faced, as capable of fomenting violence as of suppressing it. And like previous civilization theorists, Pinker does not measure those forces, so it is impossible to determine if violence declines when they rise, or rises when they decline. Third, although historical forces affect our minds and bodies, as Pinker argues, contemporary primatology, neurology, and endocrinology, rather than evolutionary psychology, may hold the best keys to understanding how circumstances affect the human body and its hormone levels in ways that have the capacity to facilitate or deter aggression.

The Up-and-Down Nature of the History of Violence

As other scholars have observed, Pinker goes to great lengths to counter the impression that the first half of the twentieth century was one of the most violent periods in known human history. He argues that many violent events in the distant past killed humans at a higher rate per 100,000 than World War I, World War II, the Russian Civil War, the Chinese Civil War, the Chinese Revolution, or the Belgian occupation of the Congo. But note that Pinker compares each of these events individually with earlier events that occurred over many years, such as the annihilation of Amerindians, the Mideast slave trade, or the Atlantic slave trade.

He also concludes, following a labored, 22-page statistical argument, that wars are causally and temporally "independent" of one another, which allows him to claim that the imperial conflicts of the late nineteenth and early twentieth century had nothing to do with World War I, which had nothing to do with the Russian or Chinese civil wars, which had nothing to do with World War II or the Chinese Revolution. This is an argument no historian would accept, and with good reason. Once we look at the imperial crises, conflicts, and collapses from the 1890s to the end of the Korean War as a single event triggered by an intense wave of globalization, state formation, empire building, and anticolonial rebellion, comparable in length to the other episodes of violence that Pinker discusses, the first half of the twentieth century assumes its rightful place as one of the deadliest in human history. And given the unreliability of the sources on previous deadly events, such as the An Lushan revolt in eighth-century China and the Mongol conquests of the thirteenth century, the first half of the twentieth century may well have been the deadliest half century in human history, not only in the number of humans killed, but in the proportion of humanity killed.

Pinker's figure 5–13 bears this out. It shows that warfare took far few lives per capita in Europe in the late medieval period (a peak of 10 to 20 per 100,000 per year) than in the early modern period (180 per 100,000), the age of democratic revolution (90 per 100,000), or the early twentieth century (250 per 100,000). Pinker's own evidence turns the civilization thesis on its head.[4]

The same problems appear if we focus on the history of homicide. The evidence for a long-term decline in murder is not there. If we look at Manuel Eisner's latest compilation of the homicide data that have been gathered by historians of Europe (Figure 8.1), we can see that there was no long-term,

Figure 8.1 Homicide rates in Europe, 1200–1830. Source: Manuel Eisner, "Long-Term Trends in Homicide Rates in Europe," available through the Historical Violence Database, sponsored by the Criminal Justice Research Center at Ohio State University, https://cjrc.osu.edu/research/interdisciplinary/hvd (accessed 15 March 2018). Outlying homicide rates omitted: Germany, 1407 (190); and Florence, 1350–1352 (152), and 1353–1355 (128).

downward trend in homicide rates between the thirteenth century and the early seventeenth century.[5] There were instead two surges in homicide: one in the half century following the Black Death (1346–1425) and one in the late sixteenth and early seventeenth centuries. This shows that the High Middle Ages (1200–1346) was not a period of extreme violence. These data also understate homicide rates in the early modern period, because those rates are based for the most part on the study of indictment rolls, rather than on the full medieval complement of legal and coroners' records, as discussed in Sara Butler's chapter for this volume.[6]

When we look in detail at places that were extremely violent during the medieval period, we discover that the problem was not impulsive violence, but calculated violence. Consider, for instance, the motives for homicides in Bedfordshire, England, one of the most violent counties that scholars have examined to date in medieval England. It had a homicide rate of around 25 per 100,000 persons per year in the mid-thirteenth century. Its coroners' rolls record 187 cases from 1265 to 1272. All but eight of the inquests include substantial information on the motive and circumstance of the homicide.[7] Were these homicides impulsive?

There were 25 homicides resulting from impulsive violence: 3 from tavern brawls, 19 from spontaneous quarrels, and 3 from long-standing grudges. There was not much family violence: only 5 spouse murders, 2 murders of persons intervening in marital disputes, 6 murders of relatives, and 2 murders of unrelated persons living within the same household. Robberies claimed the lives of half of all victims: 93 people, 82 of whom died in home invasions and 8 in highway robberies. Nine people were ambushed on paths or byways by strangers and left for dead. Three people died in sexual assaults. Another 18 victims (10 percent) were killed in "legal" homicides that involved resisting arrest, resisting attachments of property, or engaging in vigilante violence against murderers who escaped justice by claiming sanctuary and abjuring the realm. Another 16 victims (9 percent) were killed in property disputes; they died defending their property or asserting their claims to property.

Together, robberies, ambushes, and sexual assaults claimed the lives of 107 victims (60 percent). There was nothing impulsive about these homicides: they were calculated and predatory. Lack of respect for the legal system and lack of faith in its ability to bring felons to justice or resolve property disputes fairly claimed another 34 victims (19 percent). These homicides were not impulsive, but defensive. This was not a county in which individuals engaged very often in impulsive violence: this was a society in which law and order had broken down, in which the state was too weak to bring people to justice or to defend life and property, in which government (and the criminal justice system in particular) lacked legitimacy. It was a "nation-building" problem, not a personality problem or a "civilization" problem.

Note that the decline in homicide in Europe took place in the mid-seventeenth century and was not gradual, but sudden. This was when modern nations began to form, when citizens were united not merely by the power of stronger central governments, but by a number of other factors:

1. The belief that government is stable and that its legal and judicial institutions are unbiased and will redress wrongs and protect lives and property.

2. A feeling of trust in government and the officials who run it, and a belief in their legitimacy.

3. Patriotism, empathy, and fellow feeling arising from racial, religious, or political solidarity.

4. The belief that the social hierarchy is legitimate, that one's position in society is or can be satisfactory, and that one can command the respect of others without resorting to violence.

As historians will be quick to recognize, these are the key elements of successful modern polities. Whenever these elements have been in place over the past 450 years, people have been more willing to cooperate and sacrifice for the good of the whole, and homicide rates have been low. But when these elements have been missing, and people truly did not trust their governments to protect them and their interests, they have been more contentious, and in extreme cases, more power-hungry and predatory. In such circumstances, homicide rates among unrelated adults reached catastrophic levels.[8]

Notice too that whenever modern nations broke down during revolutions, civil wars, or hostile military occupations, or on contested frontiers, homicide rates jumped immediately back to the levels that Europe endured after the Black Death or during the political upheavals of the late sixteenth and early seventeenth centuries. Eisner's graph does not include data from nations that experienced political instability during the age of revolution. According to Howard Brown's study of revolutionary France, fragmentary records reveal that the rate of everyday homicides during the later years of the revolution (1795–1801) reached at least 30 per 100,000 in the four provinces he studied—and he believes the homicide rate during the early years of the revolution was much higher.[9]

Every period of political instability in nineteenth-century France (1830–1831, 1848–1850, 1870–1871) saw a spike in homicides. Homicide rates rose not just in places that were engulfed in revolutionary violence, but in places remote from such violence. As Roger Gould discovered, the homicide rate spiked in the same years even on the island of Corsica, where there were no politically motivated homicides, only an increase in feud violence and honor killings.[10]

In England, the frustration of the democratic aspirations of working people in the wake of the Napoleonic Wars led to a doubling of the homicide rate after the massacre of voting rights demonstrators at Peterloo in 1819 and to a sustained high rate through the years of Chartist agitation. But when the Second Reform Act passed in 1867, enfranchising property-less household heads in urban areas, the homicide rate fell suddenly by half; and when the Third Reform Act passed in 1884, enfranchising property-less household heads in rural areas, the homicide rate fell suddenly by half again.[11]

Also revealing are homicide rates since the end of the Cold War in nations in the former Eastern Bloc (Figure 8.2). Political instability coincided with a sudden jump in homicide rates to premodern levels (12–18 per 100,000 persons per year) in most of the European states of the former Soviet Union, and to catastrophic levels in the three nations with the highest proportions of ethnic Russians: the Russian Federation, Latvia (half Russian), and Estonia (one-third Russian). They had rates from 25 to 33 per 100,000 per year after the collapse of the former Soviet Union. (Note that Lithuania, which is only 9 percent Russian, had a homicide rate that peaked at a much lower rate: only 13 per 100,000.)[12] It will take years of research to be certain, but there is little doubt that the collapse of the Soviet Union was most keenly felt by ethnic Russians, many of whom felt powerless, unrepresented, bitter, and betrayed. But those nations in Eastern Europe that experienced the most peaceful and successful transitions to capitalism and representative democracy—Poland, Slovakia, and the Czech Republic—saw their homicides

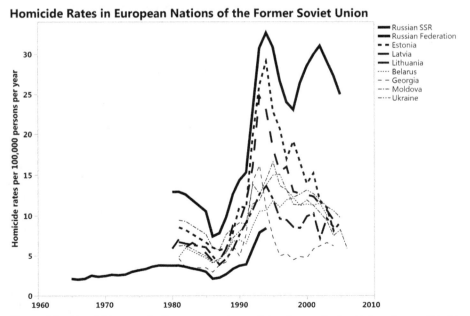

Homicide Rates in European Nations of the Former Soviet Union

Figure 8.2 Homicide rates in European nations of the former Soviet Union. Source: World Health Organization mortality data. Data for Georgia supplemented by data from United Nations Survey of Crime.

decline rapidly after a brief bump up in the early 1990s. Again, the nation-building thesis fits the data better than the civilization thesis.

We should also consider the impact of modern medicine: emergency services, trauma centers, surgery, wound care, antisepsis, antibiotics, and fluid replacement. The research is still in its infancy, but it appears that roughly half of all homicide victims in the medieval period would have survived today because of advances that were made between the 1850s and the 1950s. The impact of improvements since the 1950s has been overstated, but there is no question that the advances that occurred from the Crimean War through World War II had a dramatic impact on survival rates from life-threatening assaults.[13]

There is thus little quantitative evidence that medieval people were more impulsive and less capable of controlling their emotions than people today, a point that humanistic medieval historians have made again and again in recent years.[14] There is simply no evidence that the modern economy, the modern state, modern manners, or modern science have had any long-term impact on the predisposition to violence. When nation building is successful, in countries as different as post–World War II England, Napoleon's France, and Mussolini's Italy, homicide rates tend to be low. But when nation building fails, Europeans today are as capable as ever of interpersonal violence. The spread of literacy, refined manners, and involvement in national and international economic markets has not made a difference. When states break down or lose their legitimacy, homicide can be as serious a problem as it has ever been in the past.

The Janus Faces of the Forces that Shape History

As Reinhold Niebuhr argued eloquently in *The Irony of American History*, history does not always flow in the direction that humans intend.[15] Good can lead to evil, and evil to good, in ways we cannot foresee. There is no question that Pinker has a wonderful sense of irony, which shines through in his humor and in his thoughts on contemporary events. But his history of violence, because it strains to see his five drivers of history as progressive forces, does not have as strong a sense of irony. I am not suggesting that Pinker is unaware that Leviathan, commerce, feminization, cosmopolitanism, and reason can have unforeseen consequences, and that they can sometimes increase violence. But he downplays those consequences in his narrative in ways that undermine the accuracy of his history.

Strong European states, for instance, which had the power to tax and raise large, technologically advanced armies, increased the death rate in warfare from the medieval period to the early twentieth century. It may prove that the creation of weapons of mass destruction—atomic, chemical, and biological—will deter warfare forever between strong states with much to lose. But that is quite different from saying that strong states have deterred violence.

The same goes for Pinker's other major drivers of history. The global exchange of goods and services has led not only to cooperative, mutually advantageous exchanges, but to slavery, colonization, dispossession, and deadly international rivalries over markets and resources. Cosmopolitanism has led some people to suspect those who seem better educated and more successful than their fellow citizens and who have international or transnational as well as national loyalties. That kind of suspicion contributed mightily to the Ottoman genocide against the Armenians and the Holocaust against European Jews. Reason has led humanity not only to great scientific advances and an appreciation for evidence and careful thought, but also to ideologies whose advocates are utterly convinced that they, and not their adversaries, are the devotees of reason, data, and the scientific method. Pinker's determination to draw clear lines between reason and ideology, between the Enlightenment and Counter-Enlightenment, simply cannot stand up to historical scrutiny: they depend on each other, and grow out of each other.

Feminization, on the other hand, may hold great promise in deterring violence, but the campaign for gender equality is far from won at this point, so it is hard to be sure what its long-term impact on violence will be. What is troubling, however, is that in the United States, sexual assaults and lethal violence against women have increased, at least in the short run, whenever the balance of power has shifted toward women, as it did in the 1830s and 1840s, and as it did again in the 1960s and early 1970s. Men who accepted, embraced, or at least tolerated the growing power of women within society and intimate relationships may well have become less violent, but men who could not change or refused to change became more violent and, in a growing number of incidents, lethally violent. Pinker gets around this problem by beginning his time series on violence against women in the United States in the mid-1970s, which leaves the false impression that women's gains were never contested.[16]

But perhaps more important, civilization theorists, including Pinker, never quantify the forces that they believe have made human societies less violent; neither have they demonstrated that retreats of those forces have coincided with periods of "decivilization" and rising violence. Did states weaken, commerce decline, cosmopolitanism disappear, the standing of women deteriorate, and science lose its luster when homicide rates rose across the Western world in the 1960s and 1970s? Perhaps. But where is the evidence? The data?

The situation is different for the nation-building hypothesis. The data show, for instance, a strong correlation in nineteenth-century United States between the use of hate speech (a proxy for the decline of fellow feeling) and increases in homicide. The data show a strong correlation in the nineteenth century between the ups and downs of the homicide rate and the use of hate speech directed at African Americans and their sympathizers (the N-word) and at slave owners and their sympathizers (the "slave power"). The data show a strong correlation from colonial times into the twentieth

century between increases in the proportion of new counties in any decade named after national heroes—a proxy for faith in government and
patriotic feeling—and declines in homicide. The data show that there was
a strong correlation in the seventeenth and eighteenth centuries between
high rates of everyday homicides and the number of individuals banished,
exiled, or executed for treason or sedition—a measure of political instability and of challenges to the legitimacy of government—and the number of
deadly riots and rebellions involving contests for political power or protests
against the abuse of power by the government or its officials. There was
also a strong correlation between everyday homicides and the number of
individuals banished, exiled, or executed for heresy, witchcraft, or moral offenses (adultery, bestiality, pederasty, etc.)—a measure of hostility, division,
and distrust within communities—and deadly riots that sought to regulate
the behavior of members of the community. And the increase in homicides
of intimate partners in the early nineteenth century coincided with an increase in the number of articles in American serials that rejected the idea
that women should be subordinate to their husbands in marriage and in the
household—a measure of the degree to which male domination was being
challenged.

I do not fault Pinker for failing to develop these measures. That is a
job for historians, not for a psychologist who has brought psychological so-
phistication to the study of the history of violence. But it is troubling that
civilization theorists, unlike nation-building theorists, feel no obligation to
put their thesis at risk against quantitative measures of the forces that they
believe drive the history of violence.

Do Primatology, Neurology, and Endocrinology Hold the Keys to Understanding the Ups and Downs of Violence?

I have written elsewhere about the relationship between biology and the
history of homicide, so I will briefly state my concerns about the limitations
of the evolutionary psychology at the heart of *Better Angels*. Pinker's grasp
of human psychology is extraordinary and in line with the work of distinguished primatologists like Franz de Waal, who have concluded, as Pinker
has, that humans are "bipolar"—that is, capable of being extremely cooperative and forbearing on the one hand, and competitive and aggressive on the
other.[17] However, cutting-edge research in primatology, neurology, and endocrinology has yielded new insights into how primates, including humans,
respond physically to social situations that are likely to lead to violence, such
as political instability, destabilization of status hierarchies, and encounters
with strangers. In such situations (experimental for humans, observational
and experimental for monkeys and apes), primates generally secrete higher
levels of hormones that facilitate violence, like testosterone and cortisol, and
lower levels of hormones that deter violence, such as serotonin and oxyto-

cin. And when social conditions decrease the probability of violence, hormones return to their former levels.

Hormones do not cause violence directly, but they increase the likelihood and the severity of violence and in the aggregate can lead to higher rates of fatal and near-fatal encounters. Going forward, the key will be not simply to study humanity's inner demons and better angels, but to examine the physical responses to historical situations that may determine whether demons or angels win out.

I want to emphasize again my admiration for *Better Angels of Our Nature*. While I disagree with it, it has made an extraordinary contribution to our understanding of human psychology, and it is a remarkable synthesis of the literature on the civilization thesis. It is necessary, however, to approach the history of violence more critically, to test the civilization thesis with greater humanistic and social scientific rigor, and to explore the ways in which scientists in fields other than psychology are deepening our understanding of violence.

Acknowledgments

The author would like to thank the National Science Foundation, the Harry Frank Guggenheim Foundation, and the National Endowment for the Humanities for their support.

Randolph Roth is Professor of History and Sociology at Ohio State University. He is the author of the award-winning American Homicide *(Belknap Press of Harvard University Press, 2009). He is currently completing a history of homicides of or by children in the United States from colonial times to the present.*

Notes

1. Pieter Spierenberg, *A History of Murder: Personal Violence in Europe from the Middle Ages to the Present* (Cambridge: Polity, 2008); and Norbert N. Elias, *The Civilizing Process*, trans. E. Jephcott, 2 vols. (New York: Pantheon, 1982). The theory has been elaborated by Manuel Eisner, "Modernization, Self-Control, and Lethal Violence: The Long-Term Dynamics of European Homicide Rates in Theoretical Perspective," *British Journal of Criminology* 41, no. 4 (2001): 618–638. Historians of the United States have contributed to this theory with discussions of the civilizing influence of schools, factories, and police forces in cities in the late nineteenth century. See, for example, Roger Lane, *Violent Death in the City: Suicide, Accident, and Murder in Nineteenth-Century Philadelphia* (Cambridge, MA: Harvard University Press, 1979); Eric H. Monkkonen, *Murder in New York City* (Berkeley: University of California Press, 2001); and Steven Mennell, *The American Civilizing Process* (Montreal: McGill-Queen's University Press, 2001).

2. Steven Pinker, *Better Angels of Our Nature: Why Violence Has Declined* (New York: Viking, 2011), xxv, 482–670.
3. Pinker, *Better Angels*, xxv–xxvi.
4. Ibid., 195, 200–222, 230.
5. See Manuel Eisner, "Long-Term Trends in Homicide Rates in Europe," available through the Historical Violence Database, sponsored by the Criminal Justice Research Center at Ohio State University, https://cjrc.osu.edu/research/interdisciplinary/hvd (accessed 15 March 2018).
6. Estimating medieval homicide rates is difficult, but it is likely, as Manuel Eisner's data show, that homicide rates were lower in the thirteenth century and the early fourteenth century than in the wake of the Black Death. See Randolph Roth, "Estimates of County and Borough Populations in England, 1200–1589," "Homicide Rates in Medieval England," "Homicide Rates in Bedfordshire, 1265–1275," and the accompanying data files, available through the Historical Violence Database, sponsored by the Criminal Justice Research Center at Ohio State University, https://cjrc.osu.edu/research/interdisciplinary/hvd/europe/medieval-england. On the understatement of homicide rates in early modern England, see Randolph Roth, "Homicide in Early Modern England, 1549–1800: The Need for a Quantitative Synthesis," *Crime, History, and Societies* 5, no. 2 (2001): 33–67.
7. See Roth, "Homicide Rates in Bedfordshire."
8. Randolph Roth, *American Homicide* (Cambridge, MA: Harvard University Press, 2009).
9. Harold Brown, *Ending the Revolution: Violence, Justice, and Repression from the Terror to Napoleon* (Charlottesville: University of Virginia Press, 2006), 16–19, 98–105, and 361; and Roth, *American Homicide*, 145–146.
10. Roger V. Gould, *Collision of Wills: How Ambiguity about Social Rank Breeds Conflict* (Chicago: University of Chicago Press, 2003), 150–161; and Jean-Claude Chenais, *Histoire de la Violence en Occident de 1800 à Nos Jours*, rev. ed. (Paris: Robert Laffot, 1982), 73–85.
11. Roth, *American Homicide*, 297.
12. The data are from the World Health Organization Mortality Database, http://www.who.int/healthinfo/mortality_data/en/ (accessed 15 March 2018). The data for Georgia are supplemented by data from the United Nations Survey of Crime, Crime and Criminal Justice Data, https://www.unodc.org/unodc/en/data-and-analysis/crime-and-criminal-justice.html (accessed 15 March 2018). To adjust for undercounting by the WHO homicide data for Georgia, the UN data, for 1990–2004, were spliced with the WHO homicide data, which were multiplied by 1.49. The data in the graph are in "Homicide in Russia and the European Nations of the Former Soviet Union, 1902–2006," available through the Historical Violence Database (as above) (accessed 15 March 2018).
13. Randolph Roth, "Are Modern and Early Modern Homicide Rates Comparable? The Impact of Non-Emergency Medicine," unpublished paper, Social Science History Association, Chicago, IL, 15–18 November 2007; and Douglas Eckberg, "Trends in Conflict: Uniform Crime Reports, the National Crime Victimization Surveys, and the Lethality of Violent Crime," *Homicide Studies* 19, no. 1 (2014): 58–87.
14. See, for example, Barbara A. Hanawalt, *The Ties that Bound: Peasant Families in Medieval England* (New York: Oxford University Press, 1986); and Barbara H.

Rosenwein, *Emotional Communities in the Early Middle Ages* (Ithaca, NY: Cornell University Press, 2006).

15. Reinhold Niebuhr, *The Irony of American History* (New York: Charles Scribner's Sons, 1952).

16. Roth, *American Homicide*, 250–290, 322–325; and Pinker, *Better Angels*, 394–415.

17. Randolph Roth, "Biology and the Deep History of Homicide," *British Journal of Criminology* 51, no. 3 (2011): 535–555; and Randolph Roth, "Emotions, Facultative Adaptation, and the History of Homicide," *American Historical Review* 119, no. 5 (2014): 1529–1546. See also, for example, Franz de Waal, *Our Inner Ape: A Leading Primatologist Explains Why We Are Who We Are* (New York: Riverhead Books, 2005).

Chapter 9

The Rise and Rise of Sexual Violence

Joanna Bourke

Violent practices, technologies, and symbols increasingly permeate our everyday lives. This is the fact that Pinker seeks to debunk. He attempts to do so in five ways: by selectively choosing his data; minimizing certain harms; adopting an evolutionary psychology approach; ignoring new forms of aggression; and failing to acknowledge the political underpinnings of his own research. In this chapter, I will explore these shortcomings in relation to sexual violence.

The study of sexual violence is inherently difficult. We do not know how many people are victims, or how many are perpetrators. Every statistical database has flaws. Pinker chose to rely on the US Bureau of Justice Statistics' National Crime Victimization Survey (NCVS). This is highly problematic because the sample used by the NCVS excludes some groups who are most at risk of sexual assault, including "persons living in military barracks and institutional settings such as correctional or hospital facilities, and persons who are homeless," as well as "persons living in group quarters, such as dormitories, rooming houses, and religious group dwellings."[1] The exclusion of prisoners is particularly telling, since Pinker reports positively on increased incarceration rates in the United States, stating that one of the reasons for the decline of rape is that more "first-time rapists" have been put "behind bars."[2] Indeed, the level of incarceration in the United States is exceptional, with one in every 37 adults under some form of "correctional supervision."[3] Incarceration is not "race-blind": African Americans are imprisoned at more than five times the rate of whites.[4] Given that sexually violent men are unlikely to give up their practices, as levels of incarceration have increased dramatically, so too have levels of sexual assault in prisons. The NCVS does not record such increases in prison-based sexual violence: some violated bodies are not valued as highly as others.

Pinker could have supplemented his use of NCVS data with other sources that present a very different picture. Even if we ignore the fact that Pinker's statistics for sexual violence are drawn from British and American sources (while the World Health Organization finds that 35 percent of women worldwide have experienced either physical or sexual violence),[5] nevertheless, *reported* rapes are increasing dramatically. Between 1985 and 2007, rapes reported to the British police increased from 1,842 to 13,133. According to data released by HM Inspectorate of Constabulary on behalf of its rape-monitoring group, in 2015–2016, police recorded 23,851 reports of adults being raped.[6] In France, there was a fourfold increase in the same period (from 2,823 to 10,128).[7]

Pinker's response to the increase in reported rape might well be that the statistics actually prove his point: people are becoming more disapproving of sexual violence and less fearful of reporting assault. There is little evidence for this. Barriers to reporting sexual violence are still formidable. One survey of 1,007 women in 11 UK cities found that a startling 91 percent of women failed to report their abuse,[8] while the Rape Crisis Federation of England and Wales found that only 12 percent of the 50,000 women who contacted their services in 1998 reported the crime of rape to the police.[9] Even the NCVS found that, between 1992 and 2000, 63 percent of completed rapes, 65 percent of attempted rapes, and 74 percent of completed and attempted sexual assaults against females were not reported to the police.[10] The British Crime Survey found even lower levels of reportage: less than 20 percent of rape victims told the police.[11] Nonreportage is particularly high among minority women, the poor and disenfranchised, prostitutes, and women who are perceived as being unattractive. It is also a problem for married women who have been victimized by their partners: lack of money and access to alternative housing, in addition to emotional dependency and concerns over retaining access to children, mean that victims often feel unable to pursue prosecution.

The second trap that Pinker falls into is the minimization of certain harms. He does this, in part, by failing to understand history. He states that "one has to look long and hard through history and across cultures to find an acknowledgement of the harm of rape *from the viewpoint of the victim.*"[12] This is not the case. Rape was a heinous act precisely because it was known to inflict serious harm to victims. Medical jurisprudence textbooks were full of descriptions of the harm caused by rape, claiming (in the words of Alfred Swaine Taylor in his influential *Medical Jurisprudence* of 1861), that victims could "sustain all the injury, morally and physically, which the perpetration of the crime can possibly bring down upon her."[13]

The language used to articulate that harm was different in earlier periods, however. Prior to the 1860s, victims of *any* form of violence would not have used the word "trauma" to refer to their emotional or psychological responses. That concept was invented by John Eric Erichsen, professor of surgery at University College Hospital in London, in 1866.[14] However, victims had other languages to communicate their pain. When the aftereffects of rape were discussed, attention was paid to physical and moral realms. Women would "mysteriously waste away, sicken, grow pale, thin, waxen, and finally quit the earth, and send their forms to early graves—like blasted fruit falling before half ripened," as one author explained the aftermath of "forced love" or marital rape in 1869.[15] Victims regularly referred to "insensibility" to convey their distress. Rape victims were described as "in a state of fever" (1822);[16] "very ill, after lying in a fainting state some time" (1866);[17] they were in a "state of prostration" (1877).[18] These are very different ways to acknowledge the "harm of rape from the point of view of the victim," but powerful ones indeed for their times.

There is another way Pinker minimizes harms. He contributes to rape myths by recycling long-standing prejudices about the prevalence of false accusations. The belief that "women lie" about sexual assault is deeply embedded in our society, particularly within police forces and criminal justice systems. For example, one 2008 survey of 891 police officers in the southeastern United States found that more than 50 percent believed that half of women who complained of rape were liars and 10 percent believed that the majority of complainants were lying.[19] Police "unfound" (US) or "no-crime" (UK) large numbers of rape complaints without investigation.[20] According to a recent study by legal expert Corey Rayburn Yung, US police departments "substantially undercounted reported rapes."[21] Police departments generated "paper reductions in crime" in three ways: they designated an incident as "unfounded" without carrying out any (or any thorough) investigation; classified a reported incident as a lesser offense; and omitted to "create a written report that a victim made a rape complaint."[22] Yung concluded that the number of police jurisdictions where undercounting took place had actually increased by over 61 percent between 1995 and 2012.[23]

Pinker seems to share police skepticism about the veracity of rape complainants and the weight that should be given to women's accounts of assault. He informs readers that rape is "notoriously underreported, and at the same time often overreported (as in the highly publicized but ultimately disproven 2006 accusation against three Duke University lacrosse players)."[24] Such moral equivalence is not only wrong, it is dangerous. The extent of false accusations has generated a vast amount of academic research. In 2000–2003, for example, the UK Home Office commissioned a comprehensive research project into the problem. Initially, the researchers concluded that 9 percent of reported rape accusations were false. However, on closer analysis, this percentage dropped dramatically. They found that many of the cases listed as "no evidence of assault" were the result of someone other than the victim making the accusation. In other words, a policeman or passerby might see a woman distressed or drunk, with her clothes ripped, and report it as a suspected rape. However, when the woman was able to provide an account for what happened, she stated that no assault had taken place. In other instances, a woman regained consciousness in a public place or at home and, unable to recall what happened, worried about whether she might have been assaulted. The woman might approach the police not in order to claim rape, but to check whether any crime had been committed. Once such cases had been eliminated from the study, only 3 percent of allegations should have been categorized as false.[25] These statistics are in line with other studies.[26] Contrary to the notion that men are at risk of being falsely accused, it is significantly more common for actual rapists to get away with their actions.

Pinker's claim, therefore, that rape is overreported not only misstates the known facts but also has real-life consequences: it bolsters the view that women are prone to lie about being raped, influences the way the legal system processes rape cases, and prejudices perceptions of victims from the moment they report being raped to the time they give evidence in court.

One of the reasons Pinker may underestimate the effect of repeating rape myths is because he believes that women who report being sexually abused are now treated with care and respect. "Today," he writes, "every level of the criminal justice system has been mandated to take sexual assault seriously."[27] This is a classic case of conflating regulation with implementation. The law enforcement and justice systems may be mandated to take rape seriously, but that does not mean much in actual practice. A study by Kimberly A. Lonsway, Susan Welch, and Louise F. Fitzgerald found that sensitivity training and education about rape improved the superficial behavior of police officers, but not their attitudes toward rape victims.[28] Indeed, argues James F. Hodgskin, changes in police procedures are often simply a form of "impression management," while "internal operations, for the most part, go unchanged and unchallenged."[29] Complaints about treatment by the police and in the courts are routine.[30] As noted above, even today substantial proportions of policemen and women do not take complainants' reports seriously. Rape complainants in some US jurisdictions are routinely given polygraph tests, a procedure that would be unimaginable for any other victim of crime.[31] In recent years, women who report being sexually assaulted or raped to the police risk finding themselves charged with "perverting the course of justice."[32] In 2017, there was evidence that the forensic samples taken from tens of thousands of rape victims were never even sent for testing.[33] Conviction rates are low and declining. In the UK in 1977, one in three reported rapes resulted in a conviction. By 1985, the figure was one in five and by 1996 had fallen to one in ten.[34] Today, only one in twenty reported rapes result in a conviction. If people today abhor sexual violence more intensely than in the past, why are prosecution rates declining so precipitously?

Pinker also claims that no one now "argues that women *ought* to be humiliated at police stations and courtrooms, that husbands have a right to rape their wives, or that rapists should prey on women in apartment stair-wells and parking garages."[35] Putting these three scenarios in the same sentence creates a misleading impression. No one has ever argued that "rapists should prey on women in apartment stairwells and parking garages." However, until a few decades ago, many people did publicly argue that wives did not have the right to refuse to consent to sexual intercourse with their husbands. As late as 1991, a robust justification of the marital rape exemption was published in the *New Law Journal* by the distinguished legal academic Glanville Williams. In Williams's words:

> We are speaking of a biological activity, strongly baited by nature, which is regularly and pleasurably performed on a consensual basis by mankind . . . Occasionally some husband continues to exercise what he regards as his right when his wife refuses him, the refusal most probably resulting from the fact that the pair have had a tiff. What is wrong with his demand is not so much the act requested, but its timing, or the manner of the demand.[36]

Marital rape exemption was not abolished in England until 1992; in Greece, 2006; and it is still not a crime in more than 40 countries. There continue to be formidable difficulties for wives who report being sexually abused by their husbands.

Pinker is equally complacent about forms of sexual violence that have arisen only in the late twentieth and early twenty-first centuries: the invention and proliferation of technology-enhanced violence. He claims that the "treatment of rape in popular culture" has "changed beyond recognition" in positive ways. "Today, when the film and television industries depict a rape, it is to generate sympathy for the victim and revulsion for her attacker."[37] This is a surprising claim, given the amount of scholarship arguing that rape scenes in film and television are often included gratuitously or for titillation.

The sexualizing of violence is especially prominent in video gaming, which Pinker correctly observes is "the medium of the next generation, rivalling cinema and recorded music in revenue."[38] Pinker believes that computer games "overflow with violence and gender stereotypes" but that rape is "conspicuously absent."[39] This myth has been exploded in Anastasia Powell and Nicola Henry's book *Sexual Violence in a Digital Age*, which analyzes structural inequalities as well as the gendered harms caused by technology-facilitated sexual violence, including virtual rape, image-based sexual abuse (such as revenge pornography), and online sexual harassment.[40] Other commentators have argued that threats of rape and other attacks are routine in the genre, as is the spread of violent sexual images.[41]

Video gaming and virtual spaces are prominent examples where sexual violence is rife. In 2013, a survey of male college students found that 22 percent had engaged in technology-based sexually coercive behaviors.[42] In the virtual environment *Second Life*, users can pay to sexually assault ("grief") other characters.[43] Some popular computer games, such as *Grand Theft Auto*, include rape scenarios. In his book *Second Lives: A Journey Through Virtual*

Worlds, Tim Guest estimated that around 6.5 percent of logged-in residents have filed one or more abuse reports in *Second Life.* By the end of 2006, Linden Lab (creator of *Second Life*) was receiving "close to 2,000 abuse reports a day."[44] This is not a new phenomenon: the first recorded case of virtual rape occurred in 1993 among a cyberspace community called LambdaMOO, a multiuser, real time, virtual world. In it, a user called Mr. Bungle used his "voodoo power" to sadistically attack and rape several female characters, who were made to look as though they were enjoying it.[45] Since that time, online sexual violence has proliferated. Feminists report systemic threats of death and sexual violence. Revenge porn, when partners post sexually explicit photographs without consent, is a common ploy. Cyber harassment is also common.

Why should cybercrimes be regarded as violent? Because they have real-life effects on nonavatar people, inducing psychological disturbance (anxiety, depression, PTSD) and affecting life outcomes (sexual and social dysfunction, drug and alcohol abuse, self-harm, suicide). These forms of violence also generate major negative health outcomes for the victims' families, friends, and communities. They cause women to police their own behavior. Not only have women moved home, changed their jobs, and gone into hiding, they also "shut down their blogs, avoid websites they formerly frequented, take down social networking profiles, refrain from engaging in online political commentary, and choose not to maintain potentially lucrative or personally rewarding online presences."[46] These are real harms, not virtual ones.

Finally, Pinker's employment of an evolutionary psychology model of sexual violence is problematic. His view of sexual violence is framed in terms of self-interested competitors, a "genetic calculus," and a "reproductive spreadsheet."[47] He believes that the "prevalence of rape in human history" and the "invisibility of the victim in the legal treatment of rape" are "all too comprehensible from the vantage point of the genetic interests that shaped human desires and sentiments over the course of evolution before our sensibilities were shaped by Enlightenment humanism."[48]

He notes that "harassment, intimidation, and forced copulation are found in many species, including gorillas, orangutans, and chimpanzees."[49] Rape, he contends, "is not exactly a normal part of male sexuality [note that equivocal 'not exactly'], but it is made possible by the fact that male desire can be indiscriminate in its choice of a sexual partner and indifferent to the partner's inner life."[50] There is also a slippage from the notion that "around 5 percent of rapes result in pregnancies, which suggests that rape can be an evolutionary advantage to the rapist,"[51] to the view that this behavior was the best strategy for men in evolutionary time.

Theorists hostile to the application of evolutionary insights to modern societies will remain skeptical. It is important to note, however, that feminist evolutionary scientists have challenged the particular form of evolutionary psychology that Pinker espouses. In particular, they point out the Western, male bias of its model of reproductive strategies.[52] As Pinker is aware, "fitness" in the context of survival and reproduction is a much more complex phenomenon than his account allows for, most notably because it is affected not only by individual reproductive success in competitive environments (which may include forced sex or exploitative accumulation of material resources), but also by sexual selection (including taking into account the preferences of the opposite sex) and group selection (such as adhering to reproductive norms or restraining sexual impulses). Individual, group, and sexual selection can, and often do, work against each other. For example, a trait or behavior that can enhance sexual selection can also be nonadaptive in terms of individual fitness (for example, certain sexual display behaviors increase the risk for been preyed upon). Equally, species often behave in ways that promote the survival and reproduction of the group, at the risk of individual survival and reproduction. Evolutionary psychologists of Pinker's variety tend to focus on individual environmental and genetic interactions, while downplaying sexual selection and group selection because the latter are significantly more difficult to infer from evolutionary environments. This does not mean that individual selection is actually dominant in terms of evolutionary mechanisms. Indeed, given the logic of the evolutionary account, the scarcity of the "commodity" women possess—that is, childbearing and raising—gives particularly strong preference to female tastes in sexual selection.[53] By focusing on only one of the mechanisms of selection, Pinker's paradigm privileges a male-biased, individualistic, neoliberal account of the evolution of the brain that is primarily about self-interest rather than the group.

Furthermore, Pinker's model of reproduction fails to acknowledge the evolutionary benefits of flexible responses, which may cut across gender lines.[54] For example, primatologists have observed that primate females are often aggressive in sex and promiscuous in soliciting it.[55] Evolutionary biologist Patricia Adair Gowaty and ecologist Stephen Hubbell developed a model that emphasizes flexibility of reproductive behavior once factors such as environments, probabilities of encounters and survival, receptivity, and life history are factored in. Rather than assuming that females will be "coy" in their sexual encounters while males are promiscuous, they find that it depends on other contexts: if an individual's survival probability declines, so too will their "choosiness," whether male or female.[56] As Gowaty and Hubbell conclude, "Males, not just females, flexibly adjust choosy and indiscriminate behavior," and selection will "sometimes select against choosy females and indiscriminate males."[57]

Pinker's evolutionary approach also leads him to ignore the effect of sexual violence on certain women. He observes that rape "entangles with three parties," which he claims are "the rapist, the men who take a proprietary interest in the woman, and the woman herself."[58] He reiterates this later, when noting that the "second party to a rape is the woman's family, *particularly her father, brothers, and husband.*"[59] Pinker thus omits the effects of rape (whether actual or threatened) on the lives of all women and other vulnerable people, including mothers, sisters, and daughters of the victim.

Many of these criticisms arise from Pinker's selective use of evidence from the psychological literature. To take one example: Pinker's particular evolutionary psychological approach would predict that women would be more harmed by sexual violence than men. He cites the work of evolutionary psychologist David Buss, claiming that Buss "shows that men underestimate how upsetting sexual aggression is to a female victim, while women overestimate how upsetting sexual aggression is to a male victim."[60] In fact, Buss's research was done in the 1980s, and rather than showing a universal pattern differentiating male versus female responses, it is based on a sample of male and female undergraduates enrolled in a psychology course at a large midwestern university. Participation in the survey earned the participants credits for their course.[61] These respondents are psychology's WEIRDs (that is, Western, educated, undergraduate students from industrialized, rich, and democratic countries). Furthermore, the questions that these students were asked to respond to carried within them a strong presumption for an evolutionary account of emotional responses to abuse—an account these students would have recognized given its prominence in psychology curricula of the time. The students were directed from the start that the project was investigating "Conflict between Men and Women," as the sheet of paper they were given was titled. All these factors strongly biased the survey.

Furthermore, Pinker does not report that Buss's study failed to support the hypothesis that "women would be upset and angered by the hypothesized feature of male reproductive strategy involving sexual aggressiveness."[62] Indeed, Buss concluded that "overall, these results provide only partial support for the theory of conflict between the sexes on the basis of conflicting reproductive strategies."[63] The experiment's evolutionary theory was convincing only where students were asked to speculate on how "irritating, annoying, and upsetting" sexual aggressiveness would be to a person the man/woman was "involved with." As David Buller argues in *Adapting Minds: Evolutionary Psychology and the Persistent Quest for Human Nature,* both Pinker's and Buss's methodologies are flawed and the evidence does not support their conclusions. Buller concludes that human minds are not adapted to the Pleistocene, at either the individual or population level. Minds are continually adapting.[64]

In conclusion, Pinker fails to recognize the ideological underpinnings of his research. He is keen to accuse his critics of ideological biases, while failing to acknowledge or even notice his own neoliberal defense of Western civilization. Feminist scientists are frequently forced to defend themselves against the accusation that they allow their politics to interfere with scientific objectivity. Gowaty explained to her critics that

> science is the practice of systematic observation and experiment as a means
> to test predictions from hypotheses while reducing or eliminating (i.e. con-

trolling) the effects of perceived and possible biases on results and conclu-sions. So what it means to be self-consciously political is that one is thereby in a scientifically better position relative to those who are unaware of the political and social forces potentially affecting their science . . . Buttressed with better controls, controls against potential biases we are able to per-ceive, makes our conclusions more reliable.[65]

Like Gowaty, Pinker's project is informed by his politics. Unlike Gowaty, by failing to acknowledge and then control for his own ideological bias, Pinker has missed an opportunity to convincingly explain the changing nature of violence in our societies.

Acknowledgment

Many thanks to the Wellcome Trust for research support.

Joanna Bourke is Professor of History at Birkbeck, University of London, and Fellow of the British Academy. She is the prize-winning author of thirteen books, among them Rape: A History from the 1860s to the Present, What It Means to Be Human: Reflections from 1791 to the Present, *and* The Story of Pain: From Prayer to Painkillers. *She is the Principal Investigator in a Wellcome Trust–funded project entitled "Sexual Violence, Medicine, and Psychiatry."*

Notes

1. Bureau of Justice Statistics, "Data Collection: National Crime Victimization Study (NCVS)" (2015), https://www.bjs.gov/index.cfm?ty=dcdetail&iid=245# Methodology (accessed 1 November 2017).
2. Steven Pinker, *The Better Angels of Our Nature: A History of Violence and Humanity* (London: Penguin Books, 2011), 486.
3. NAACP, "Criminal Justice Fact Sheet," http://www.naacp.org/criminal-justice-fact-sheet/ (accessed 1 December 2017).
4. Ibid.
5. World Health Organization, *Global and Regional Estimates of Violence Against Women: Prevalence and Health Effects of and Non-Partner Sexual Violence* (Geneva: WHO, 2013), 2.
6. Vikram Dodd and Helena Bengtsson, "Reported Rapes Double in England and Wales in Four Years," *Guardian,* 13 October 2016, https://www.theguardian.com/society/2016/oct/13/reported-rapes-in-england-and-wales-double-in-five-years (accessed 1 December 2017).
7. Nicole Fayard and Yvette Rocheron, "'Moi quand on dit qu'une femme ment, eh bien, elle ment': The Administration of Rape in Twenty-First Century France and England and Wales," *French Politics, Culture and Society* 29, no. 1 (Spring 2011): 74.

8. K. Painter, *Wife Rape, Marriage and Law: Survey Report, Key-Findings and Recommendation* (Manchester: University of Manchester, Department of Social Policy and Social Work, 1991).

9. Cited in H. M. Crown Prosecution Service Inspectorate, *A Report on the Joint Inspection into the Investigation and Prosecution of Cases Involving Allegations of Rape* (London: H. M. Crown Prosecution Service Inspectorate, April 2002), 1.

10. Callie Marie Rennison, *Rape and Sexual Assault: Reporting to Police and Medical Attention, 1992–2000* (Washington, DC: Bureau of Justice Statistics, 2002), 2.

11. Andy Myhill and Jonathan Allen, *Rape and Sexual Assault of Women: The Extent and Nature of the Problem—Findings from the British Crime Survey* (London: Home Office Research, Development, and Statistics Directorate, March 2002), vii. See also MOPAC, *Sexual Violence: The London Sexual Violence Needs Assessment 2016 for MOPAC and NHS England (London)* (London: MBARC, November 2016), 26, www.london.gov.uk/sites/default/files/sexual_violence_needs_assessment_rep ort_2016.pdf.

12. Pinker, *Better Angels,* 476; emphasis in original.

13. Alfred Swaine Taylor, *Medical Jurisprudence* (London: n.p., 1861), 687–698.

14. John Eric Erichsen, *On Railway and Other Injuries of the Nervous System* (London: Walton and Maberly, 1866), 9. Also see John Eric Erichsen, *On Concussion of the Spine, Nervous Shock, and Other Obscure Injuries of the Nervous System in Their Clinical and Medico-Legal Aspects* (London: Longman, Green and Co., 1875), 195.

15. De St. Leon, *Love and Its Hidden History,* 4th ed. (Boston: William White and Co., 1869), 102.

16. "Scotland. Perth Circuit Court," *Times,* 21 September 1822.

17. "Crown Court," *Times,* 8 March 1866.

18. "Outrage," *Times,* 7 September 1877. For a broader discussion, see Joanna Bourke, *Rape: A History from the 1860s to the Present* (London: Virago, 2007).

19. Amy Dellinger Page, "Gateway to Reform? Policy Implications of Police Officers' Attitudes Towards Rape," *American Journal of Criminal Justice* 33, no. 1 (May 2008): 44–58. See also Martin D. Schwartz, "National Institute of Justice Visiting Fellowship: Police Investigation of Rape—Roadblocks and Solutions," *U.S. Department of Justice* (December 2012), http://www.ncjrs.gov/pdffiles1/nij/grants/232667.pdf (accessed 1 December 2017).

20. Lisa R. Avalos, "Policing Rape Complaints: When Reporting Rape Becomes a Crime," *Journal of Gender, Race, and Justice* 20, no. 3 (2017): 459–508, here 466–467.

21. Corey Rayburn Yung, "How to Lie with Rape Statistics: America's Hidden Rape Crisis," *Iowa Law Review* 99, no. 1 (2014): 1197–1256, here 1197.

22. Yung, "How to Lie with Rape Statistics," 1197.

23. Ibid.

24. Pinker, *Better Angels,* 484.

25. Liz Kelly, Jo Lovett, and Linda Regan, *A Gap or a Chasm? Attrition in Reported Rape Cases,* Home Office Research Study 293 (London: Home Office Research, Development and Statistics Directorate, February 2005), xi and 46–47.

26. Clare Gunby, Anna Carline, and Caryl Beynon, "Regretting It after: Focus Group Perspectives on Alcohol Consumption, Nonconsensual Sex and False Allegations of Rape," *Social and Legal Studies* 22, no. 1 (2013): 87–106, here 87 and 106; Philip N. S. Rumney, "False Allegations of Rape," *Cambridge Law Journal* 65, no. 1 (2006): 128–158; Liz Kelly, "The (In)credible Words of Women: False Allegations in European Rape Research," *Violence Against Women* 16, no. 12

(2010): 1345–1355; David Lisak, Lori Gardiner, Sarah C. Nicksa, and Ashley M. Cote, "False Allegations of Sexual Assault: An Analysis of Ten Years of Reported Cases," *Violence Against Women* 16, no. 12 (2010): 1318–1334.

27. Pinker, *Better Angels*, 482.
28. Kimberly A. Lonsway, Susan Welch, and Louise F. Fitzgerald, "Police Training in Sexual Assault Response: Process, Outcomes, and Elements of Change," *Criminal Justice and Behavior* 28, no. 6 (2001): 695–730.
29. James F. Hodgson, "Policing Sexual Violence: A Case Study of *Jane Doe v. the Metropolitan Toronto Police*," in *Sexual Violence: Policies, Practices, and Challenges in the United States and Canada*, ed. James F. Hodgson and Debra S. Kelley (Westport, CT: Praeger, 2002), 173–221, here 173.
30. For example, see MOPAC, *Sexual Violence*, 29.
31. Vivian B. Lord and Gary Rassel, "Law Enforcement's Response to Sexual Assault: A Comparative Study of Nine Counties in North Carolina," in Hodgson and Kelley, *Sexual Violence*, 166; Jeanne C. Marsh, Alison Geist, and Nathan Caplan, *Rape and the Limits of Law Reform* (Boston: Auburn House, 1982).
32. Avalos, "Policing Rape Complaints," 460–471.
33. Jill E. Daly, "Gathering Dust on the Evidence Shelves of the US," *Women's Rights Law Reporter* 25, no. 1 (2003): 17–36; Milli Kanani, "Testing Justice," *Columbia Human Rights Law Review* 42, no. 3 (2011): 943–992; Cassia Spohn, "Untested Sexual Assault Kits: A National Dilemma," *Criminality and Public Policy* 15, no. 2 (2016): 551–554; Tara Kalar, Elizabeth Meske, Alison Schimdt, and Shirin Johnson, "A Crisis of Complacency: Minnesota's Untested Rape Kit Backlog," *Bench and Bar of Minnesota* 74, no. 3 (2017): 22–28.
34. Jessica Harris and Sharon Grace, *A Question of Evidence? Investigating and Prosecuting Rape in the 1990s* (London: Home Office Research Study 196, 1999), iii.
35. Pinker, *Better Angels*, 246; emphasis in original.
36. Glanville Williams, "The Problem of Domestic Rape," *New Law Journal* 191, no. 6491 (15 February 1991): 205; and Glanville Williams, "The Problem of Domestic Rape," *New Law Journal* 191, no. 6492 (22 February 1991): 246.
37. Pinker, *Better Angels*, 483.
38. Ibid.
39. Ibid., 484.
40. Anastasia Powell and Nicola Henry, *Sexual Violence in a Digital Age* (London: Palgrave, 2016).
41. This is a huge literature, but see Jessica Valenti, "How the Web Became a Sexists' Paradise" *Guardian*, 6 April 2007, https://www.theguardian.com/world/2007/apr/06/gender.blogging (accessed 1 December 2017); Cheryl Lindsey Seelhoff, "A Chilling Effect: The Oppression and Silencing of Women Journalists and Bloggers Worldwide," *Off Our Backs* 37, no. 1 (2007): 18–21; and Catherine Holahan, "The Dark Side of Web Anonymity," *Bloomberg Businessweek*, 1 May 2008, https://www.bloomberg.com/news/articles/2008-04-30/the-dark-side-of-web-anonymity (accessed 1 December 2017).
42. Martie P. Thompson and Deidra J. Morrison, "Prospective Predictors of Technology-Based Sexual Coercion by College Males," *Psychology of Violence* 3, no. 3 (2013): 233–246.
43. Michael Bugeja, "Avatar Rape," *Inside Higher Education*, 25 February 2010, http://www.insidehighered.com/views/2010/02/25/bugeja (accessed 1 November 2017).

44. Tim Guest, *Second Lives: A Journey Through Virtual Worlds* (London: Hutchinson, 2007), 227; Melissa Mary Fenech Sander, "Questions of Accountability and Illegality of Virtual Rape," (MSc thesis, Iowa State University, 2009).

45. Julian Dibbell, "A Rape in Cyberspace," *Village Voice,* 21 December 1993, https://www. villagevoice.com/2005/10/18/special/a-rape-in-cyberspace/ (accessed 1 December 2017); and Julian Dibbell, "A Rape in Cyberspace Or How an Evil Clown, A Haitian Trickster Spirit, Two Wizards, and a Cast of Dozens Turned a Database into a Society," *Annual Survey of American Law,* 1994, 471–489. See also K. De Vries, "Avatars Out of Control," *Computers, Privacy, and Data Protection,* 2011, 233–250; G. Young and M. T. Whitty, "Games Without Frontiers," *Computers in Human Behavior* 26, no. 6 (2010): 1228; Mary Anne Franks, "Unwilling Avatars: Idealism and Discrimination in Cyberspace," *Columbia Journal of Gender and Law* 20, no. 1 (2011): 224–261; Jessica Wolfendale, "My Avatar, My Self: Virtual Harm and Attachment," *Ethics and Information Technology* 9, no. 2 (2007): 111–119.

46. For a small sample of the evidence, see Danielle Keats Citron, *Hate Crimes in Cyberspace* (Cambridge, MA: Harvard University Press, 2014); Franks, "Unwilling Avatars"; Nicola Henry and Anastasia Powell, "Embodied Harms: Gender, Shame, and Technology-Facilitated Sexual Violence," *Violence Against Women* 21, no. 6 (March 2015): 758–779; Sander, "Questions of Accountability and Illegality of Virtual Rape."

47. Pinker, *Better Angels,* 480.

48. Ibid., 477.

49. Ibid., 477.

50. Ibid., 488.

51. Ibid., 477.

52. Patricia Adair Gowaty, "Power Asymmetries Between the Sexes, Mate Preferences, and Components of Fitness," in *Evolution, Gender, and Rape,* ed. Cheryl Brown Travis (Cambridge, MA: MIT Press, 2003); Sarah Blaffer Hrdy, "'Raising Darwin's Consciousness': Female Sexuality and the Prehominid Origins of Patriarchy," *Human Nature* 8, no. 1 (1997): 1–49; Sarah Blaffer Hrdy, *The Woman that Never Evolved: With a New Preface* (Cambridge, MA: Harvard University Press, 1999); Marlene Zuk, *Sexual Selection: What We Can and Can't Learn About Sex from Animals* (Berkeley: University of California Press, 2002).

53. For further discussion, see Amy L. Wax, "Evolution and the Bounds of Human," *Law and Philosophy* 23, no. 6 (2004): 527–591, here 540.

54. See Laurette T. Liesen, "Women, Behavior, and Evolution: Understanding the Debate Between Feminist Evolutionists and Evolutionary Psychologists," *Politics and the Life Sciences* 26, no. 1 (2007): 51–70.

55. Sarah Blaffer Hrdy, "Empathy, Polyandry, and the Myth of the Coy Female," in *Conceptual Issues in Evolutionary Biology,* ed. Elliott Sober (Cambridge, MA: MIT Press, 1994), 123–129; Barbara Smuts, "The Evolutionary Origins of Patriarchy," *Human Nature* 6, no. 1 (1995): 1–32.

56. Patricia Adair Gowaty and Stephen P. Hubbell, "Chance, Time Allocation, and the Evolution of Adaptively Flexible Sex Role Behavior," *Integrative and Comparative Biology* 45, no. 5 (2005): 931–944.

57. Gowaty and Hubbell, "Chance," 940. See also Steven Gangestad and Jeffrey Simpson, "The Evolution of Human Mating: Trade-offs and Strategic Pluralism," *Behavioral and Brain Sciences* 23 (2000): 575–576.

58. Pinker, *Better Angels*, 477.
59. Ibid., 478; emphasis added.
60. Ibid., 488–489, referring to David M. Buss, "Conflict between the Sexes: Strategic Interference and the Evocation of Anger and Upset," *Journal of Personality and Social Psychology* 56, no. 5 (1989): 735–747.
61. Buss, "Conflict between the Sexes," 737.
62. Ibid., 741.
63. Ibid., 741.
64. David Buller, *Adapting Minds: Evolutionary Psychology and the Persistent Quest for Human Nature* (Cambridge, MA: MIT Press, 2005), 14.
65. Patricia Adair Gowaty, "Introduction: Darwinian Feminists and Feminist Evolutionists," in *Feminism and Evolutionary Biology: Boundaries, Intersections, and Frontiers*, ed. Patricia Adair Gowaty (New York: Chapman and Hall, 1997), 1–17, here 14.

Chapter 10

The Inner Demons of
The Better Angels of Our Nature

Daniel Lord Smail

Several decades ago, grumbling to a medieval historian in Paris after another bad experience with French bureaucracy, I asked him why his fellow citizens put up with it. In his thoughtful way, he explained that France's citizens harbor positive feelings toward the state. They tolerate the indignities in the belief that today's world, whatever its faults, is a far cry better than the feudal despotism that preceded it. I have no idea whether my colleague was an accurate witness to the state of opinion in France at the time. But even so, the anecdote is a reminder that once upon a time, historians celebrated the idea of progress and understood it as their duty to convey the virtues of Western civilization to their students and readers.

Historians, by and large, have lost this sunny sense of optimism about the possibility of progress. As a graduate student in the late 1980s, I was taught that the first serious doubts arose in the wake of the Holocaust, as historians began to confront the horrors of the Nazi era and found that they could not be squared with a belief in Western progress. The indictments mounted in the ensuing decades. But when the discipline of history retreated from the vision of progress, a vacuum was created. If you happen to believe in the values of Western civilization, who will be your champion?

In 2011, Steven Pinker took up the mantle with the publication of *The Better Angels of Our Nature*, the arguments of which he has recently developed further in *Enlightenment Now: The Case for Reason, Science, Humanism, and Progress.*[1] Both books offer a spirited defense of Western civilization and do so through the writing of history. I open my door to all who believe that the study of the past brings clarity. Like most of my colleagues in the profession, I don't believe that history belongs only to the historians. If some have bristled at Pinker's interventions, it is not because historians are inhospitable. The problem is that Pinker is indifferent to the basic tenets of academic hospitality, like a guest who tracks mud into the house, puts his feet on the table, and spills ashes on the carpet. These violations of hospitality seem peculiar, given Pinker's belief in the civilizing function of manners. Much of his recent work has an equally oxymoronic quality. He argues passionately on behalf of reason. In praise of peace, he wields prose as a weapon. Most problematically, he deploys heuristic devices—images and motifs that evoke visceral responses—in lieu of careful and reasoned analyses.

Inspired by Pinker's own dichotomy, I shall divide these remarks into two sections, the first of which addresses the better side of *Better Angels*. Like Pinker, I believe that the brain-body system is an actor in the making of history, and where Pinker draws on his own expertise in the cognitive sciences, there is much to commend in the book. But *Better Angels* is also characterized by some inner demons. These arise when his passion for his subject overwhelms his capacity to do due diligence when it comes to researching and understanding the human past.

The Better Angels of *Better Angels*

In the second half of the nineteenth century, in the wake of the time revolution that accompanied the 1859 publication of Charles Darwin's *On the Origin of Species,* the bottom dropped out from the world's chronology, leaving European historians teetering on the edge of the vast abyss of time. Nineteenth-century European cosmology was a brittle thing, so tightly strung in the time frame allotted by the Book of Genesis that the discovery of deep time should have shattered that cosmology into a thousand shards. That it did not is one of the most remarkable happenings in the history of Western historiography. Between 1850 and 1950, the short chronology of shallow history was not abandoned. Instead, it was translated into a secular key, as the origins of human history were moved from Eden to Sumer. This sleight of hand allowed Euro-American historians to avoid the difficult task of learning how to narrate human history in deep time.

In recent years, historians have begun to propose new ways to link humanity's deep past with the present.[2] At its best, *Better Angels* makes an original contribution to this literature, using the history of violence as an organizing thread. The narrative arc of *Better Angels* is defined by the trope of decline; like all narrative arcs, this one is based on quantitative claims. This brings us to one of the most interesting methodological challenges associated with the writing of deep history, namely, the fact that the evidence we use necessarily changes across the long span of human time, in the handoff from paleontology and human evolutionary biology to archaeology and history. How do we commensurate findings based on evidence drawn from independent lines of inquiry?

Pinker solves this methodological challenge by offering a single proxy for violence, namely, the rate of homicide or violent death, and then marshaling all available data, regardless of domain or methodology, in order to measure change over time. Some anthropologists have expressed reservations about the reliability of the data he uses to describe rates of violent death in the earliest historical periods, although for my part I have no serious objection to the claim that the homicide rate in later medieval Europe was high relative to today.[3] But either way, this is a good and healthy debate. To reiterate, *Better Angels* offers a bold new model for linking the many eras of the human past into a single history.

As suggested earlier, the narrative arc of *Better Angels* is defined by decline. This is not entirely accurate as a characterization, however, because Pinker also deploys a very different type of narrative explanation based on a form I shall call the "slider." Let me explain. The "better angels" and "inner demons" of the book are heuristic devices for conveying more complex ideas. The first term refers to the human capacity for cooperation, altruism, and empathy; its counterpart describes the human propensity for tribal hostility, suspicion, and violence. Both predispositions emerged in the evolutionary past.[4] But although all humans have the weird capacity to be both angels and demons at the same time, the intensity of the predisposition is variable. To a significant degree, environmental or cultural circumstances are able to play up the angels and play down the demons, or vice versa.

Now array these predispositions at the ends of a single behavioral spectrum, and add a slider that can be moved left or right, depending on biographical or historical circumstances. Any individual will be located somewhere on the spectrum. More interestingly, you can characterize whole populations by averaging the propensities of all the individuals in the group. This is a dramatically simplified reduction of a complicated situation, of course, but you get the point. The central historical explanation of *Better Angels* describes a movement of the slider from violence to peace.

From time to time, I find myself discussing this interesting argument with students and colleagues. Almost invariably, it turns out that no one gets it. The reason, I think, is that Pinker's critics often view him as a genetic determinist. But this critique is not quite accurate—at least, where *Better Angels* is concerned. The arguments of the book, instead, are built on the claim that culture matters. In particular, Pinker claims that the forces responsible for moving the slider from the demonic toward the angelic can be located in the cultural changes associated with the rise of civility, manners, and education in the West. There was nothing preordained about this, and no guarantee that the slider will remain on the angelic side. "Declines in violence," Pinker argues, "are caused by political, economic, and ideological conditions that take hold in particular cultures at particular times. If the conditions reverse, violence could go right back up."[5] Far from being a teleology, the dominant narrative of *Better Angels* is founded on contingency.

Why do some readers miss this point? To appreciate what Pinker is arguing, it helps to be familiar with the latest trends in the field of evolutionary psychology. At the risk of oversimplifying a complex and interesting subject, let me define a distinction between the evolutionary psychology of the 1990s and that of today. The earlier form, which I call Evolutionary Psychology 1.0, was based on the thesis of massive modularity. Scholars in the field assumed that many forms of human behavior are governed by hardwired modules that arose in the brain over the course of human evolution.[6] Thus, we are afraid of the dark not because the unlit basement is dangerous but instead because the ancestral night was full of leopards who ate us. The gene-centered approach to human cognition and human behavior characteristic of EP 1.0 was founded on the idea that although culture changes rapidly, genes change slowly or not at all. Blindly and dumbly, they continue to prime us to behave in an environment that no longer exists.

Given that Pinker's best-selling 1997 work *How the Mind Works* was one of the leading texts in EP 1.0, readers are not at fault for associating him with the idea that genes are destiny.[7] But unbeknownst to some of its critics, the field of evolutionary psychology has undergone a shift in recent years toward EP 2.0, which offers a more nuanced and less deterministic explanation for human behavior. Consider, by way of example, Jonathan Haidt's work of moral psychology, *The Righteous Mind*.[8] Haidt argues that all people are capable of having five moral senses. That much is a given. But the intensity of the moral sense is not fixed a priori. Instead, given cultures or environments are capable of overactivating some of the moral senses and deactivating others. By way of analogy, think of a painter who has five pigments at her disposal and uses them to greater or lesser degrees, or sometimes not at all. Since the moral senses can be activated to greater or lesser degrees, this means that every human subpopulation, and indeed every individual, has a unique moral canvas.

Historical explanation, lately, has been troubled by the difficulty of explaining how the universal fits with the particular. Scholars in the history of emotions, for example, have claimed that anything that is universal must be invisible to history, a discipline concerned with explaining change in the past. As Barbara Rosenwein has put it, "if emotions are, as many scientists think, biological entities, universal within all human populations, do they—indeed can they—have much of a history at all?"[9] Jan Plamper has acknowledged that it might well be true that emotions "possess a constant, transhistorical, and culturally generalized foundation." But since history is interested in what varies in human cultures, he argues, these universals are "uninteresting" and at best "trivially true."[10] The slider model developed by Pinker offers a device for making universals visible to historical practice. In this regard, *Better Angels* is very good to think with.

The Inner Demons of *Better Angels*

In turning to the inner demons of *Better Angels,* I shall put on the hat I wear as a historian of later medieval Europe, a period portrayed with withering scorn in *Better Angels.* Europe between the years 1250 and 1500 was a foreign country, and they did things differently there. Some of those things were admirable: for instance, their diet consisted of completely organic and locally sourced foods and no one suffered from opioid addiction. The other stuff was maybe not so admirable. But the past is past, and we study it not to hold a mirror up to ourselves but in the hopes of understanding another world on its own terms. A historian is like a naturalist who studies not only koala bears and gentle earthworms but also parasitical ichneumon wasps, slave-making ants, and infanticidal Hanuman langurs. My job is not to moralize about the unpleasant stuff I find in the past. Nearly everything in the past is capable of explanation, and explanation brings knowledge of the many ways in which humans are human.

With this in mind, consider the Middle Ages as depicted in *Better Angels*:

> Medieval Christendom was a culture of cruelty. Torture was meted out by national and local governments throughout the Continent, and it was codified in laws that prescribed blinding, branding, amputation of hands, ears, noses, and tongues, and other forms of mutilation as punishments for minor crimes. Executions were orgies of sadism, climaxing with ordeals of prolonged killing such as burning at the stake, breaking on the wheel, pulling apart by horses, impalement through the rectum, disembowelment by winding a man's intestines around a spool, and even hanging, which was a slow racking and strangulation rather than a quick breaking of the neck. Sadistic tortures were also inflicted by the Christian church during its inquisitions, witch hunts, and religious wars. Torture had been authorized by the ironically named Pope Innocent IV in 1251, and the order of Dominican monks carried it out with relish. As the *Inquisition* coffee table book notes, under Pope Paul IV (1555–59), the Inquisition was "downright insatiable— Paul, a Dominican and one-time Grand Inquisitor, was himself a fervent and skilled practitioner of torture and atrocious mass murders."[11]

Yow. It is difficult to know where to begin. On a factual level, executions in later medieval Europe were rare on a per capita basis; the same is true for judicial torture. It is not that the kind of stuff described by Pinker never happened; by the sixteenth and seventeenth centuries, it is fair to say that rates of torture and execution had risen from "rare" to "very uncommon." But a "culture of cruelty"?

So where does Pinker go wrong? He has fallen victim to the availability heuristic, where impressions that are striking and ready-to-hand in pop culture have overwhelmed his duty to deal responsibly with the literature in the field. Having no desire, however, to refute Pinker via a long historiographical survey—which Sara Butler has already done effectively in this volume—let me draw attention to the literature that Pinker has cited as evidence for this portrayal. One of the references is mentioned in the passage: a "coffee table book." Huh? The endnote refers to a source identified in the bibliography as: "Held, R. 1986. *Inquisition: A selected survey of the collection of torture instruments from the Middle Ages to our times.* Aslockton, Notts, U.K.: Avon & Arno."[12] You can do the next bit on your own: go to the Internet and try to authenticate the book's existence. In fairness, you may find a related title by Mr. Held and in this you can find a passage that is similar to the one cited.[13] But I have only this to say about the real book: it's not very good.[14] Another citation in *Better Angels* takes you to the work of an author who, alarmingly, was once a professional sword-swallower.[15] Several other citations inspire more confidence at first blush, but problems happen when you read further. A book chapter by the legal scholar Sanford Levinson, for instance, offers no support for the claims that Pinker attributes to it.[16] Most problematically, you will search *Better Angels* in vain for the formative book on European law and torture by the legal historian John Langbein, or the nuanced and thoughtful rebuttal to Langbein offered by the medieval historian Edward Peters.[17] Neither book is hard to find. Here is one of the rules of academic hospitality: when you enter another discipline, take time to cite the appropriate literature.

At a basic level, Pinker is wrong about some of his facts, at least where medieval Europe is concerned. This inattentiveness to evidence is seriously troubling in a work that otherwise extols the virtues of Western reasoning. And it raises this question: why did Pinker's predisposition to demonize the past overwhelm his duty to practice responsible scholarship? This is a real head-scratcher inasmuch as it leads to a profound inconsistency in the logic of his argument. In chapter 2, he praises "Leviathan" (p. 35), the coercive apparatus of the state, as the first of several historical forces responsible for bringing down the supposedly high levels of prehistoric violence. But then, in chapter 4, he condemns the very tools used by Leviathan, namely, torture and spectacles of execution.

Pinker is genuinely horrified by the suffering that defines the natural world (e.g., p. 32). Like a shaman, he slides readily into the bodies of other animals—the starling torn apart by the hawk; the horse tormented by insects—and feels their pain. He demonizes the past, I think, because he imagines that the human past was full of the pain and suffering typical of the natural world. In his view, history describes our long, slow escape from the nightmarish world of natural selection. Thanks to the blessed constraints of civilization, we have been rescued from the ravages of the diseases and animals that once preyed upon our bodies and from the violence of our fellow humans.

As this suggests, *Better Angels* is not a work of history. It is best understood as a work of moral and historical theology. It describes the past in terms of a neo-Augustinian vision where nature, not sin, is the source of evil, and civilization plays the role of the Savior. Not being a Christian theologian, I am in no position to delve into the book's moral claims. But on the question of whether the study of the past is compatible with moral theology, I stand with Stephen Jay Gould, who addressed the temptation to moralize the past in his 1982 essay, "Nonmoral Nature." The essay explores a question that agonized the theologians and naturalists of nineteenth-century Europe: "How could a benevolent God create such a world of carnage and bloodshed?" Gould's answer: "Nature contains no moral messages framed in human terms. Morality is a subject for philosophers, theologians, students of the humanities, indeed for all thinking people. The answers will not be read passively from nature; they do not, and cannot, arise from the data of science. The factual state of the world does not teach us how we, with our powers for good and evil, should alter or preserve it in the most ethical manner."[18] Gould's rebuttal, of course, tacitly accepts the claim that the natural world really was a world of carnage and bloodshed. But was it? Here, let us turn to the evidence that Pinker has adduced to prove that violence has declined over the millennia.

"Violence" is hard to define and even harder to measure. Pinker understands this point, which is why he used violent death as a proxy. But not all proxies are created equal, and if you lose your keys in the darkness, you are certainly not authorized to search for them under the streetlight. In a philosophical sense, imagine a dystopian world in which all people are imprisoned in physical or mental shackles and therefore incapable of violent acts: a spectacularly violent world in which the rate of violent death is zero. More realistically, consider a society in which human slaves are procured and treated with brutality—shackled, whipped, raped, humiliated, subjected to social death—but pains are taken to ensure that they don't die. As these scenarios indicate, violent death is not a suitable proxy for violence.

The semantic narrowing of "violence" arises because Pinker often associates violent acts with (male) genetic predispositions, in this case operating through the rage circuitry and other organs of violence.[19] The problems here are obvious. To take an example, any objective measurement of pain and suffering would conclude that the American meat-packing industry is violent.[20] Apart from a brief section concerned with animals (465–473), however, Pinker's definition of violence is primarily restricted to humans. Beyond that—and with the major exception of war deaths—it is concerned only with forms of violence processed by the criminal justice system. Given this bias, Pinker defines violence according to a vector that proceeds from the aggressor to the victim. The victim, in this scenario, is passive and invisible.

Now think about this very carefully: why should we accept an understanding of violence centered on the brain circuitry of the aggressor rather than that of the victim? Taking a victim-centered perspective would allow us to consider the micro- and macroaggressions that make the present day feel violent to African Americans and other minority groups, not to mention the forms of slow or structural violence that operate against the poor.[21] It would allow us to include the fact that many women experience forms of nonlethal violence in the workplace and elsewhere in the public sphere. I am not claiming that these kinds of violence have increased in the last century. My claim is that the decline in violent death since the Middle Ages may seem less important when measured against a baseline comparison of the enduring forms of structural violence. However awful violent death might be, after all, it is experienced at a rate far lower than the routine injuries and humiliations of structural violence.

If we define violence from the victims' point of view, the appropriate measure of violence will be their quantum of pain and humiliation. I can readily imagine the objection to this: pain and suffering, in past societies, are not directly measurable. *But neither is violence.* And since we have to use proxies anyway, why not use a victim-centered proxy, such as evidence for chronic stress? In the twentieth century, chronic stress can be measured through simple proxies such as life span, obesity, heart disease, and rates of opioid addiction.[22] What we learn is that chronic stress is associated with poverty and the condition of being disempowered. Crucially, what may matter is not absolute poverty but relative poverty. As Amartya Sen pointed out in 1999, African Americans as a whole are wealthier than the inhabitants of the state of Kerala in India. But Sen reports that the health outcomes of African Americans are worse than those of the Keralans, a situation arising from their condition of relative poverty.[23] If what matters is relative rather than absolute poverty, there are grounds for believing that structural violence has increased over the last half millennium.

And now to perhaps the most important question of all: why should it matter that violence has declined? At the heart of *Better Angels,* you will find the idea that people are safer now than they were in the past, and for that reason they are happier. Or at least, people *ought* to be happier, and would be so if those dang historians would do their job and acknowledge the facts. But this argument fails to account for one of the most important findings of recent decades of research in the psychology of well-being. We are accustomed to the world we inhabit, and our measures of happiness and contentment are defined by the parameters of the possible in the present day. Our subjective well-being is anchored at a set point determined by our personality traits.[24] Life events—winning the lottery, suffering injury in an accident—will cause feelings of happiness to wax or wane.[25] But a kind of psychological elastic constantly pulls us back to our set point.

Contrary to what Pinker suggests, subjective well-being is not determined by intermittent experiences such as violence. It is determined largely by the attachments we form with family, friends, and things. The subjective well-being of a man or woman living long ago, in the Pleistocene, would have been determined by the experience of living in a warm and supportive social environment, and not by the group's objective state of poverty, or the dangers of the night, or violent events. The personality traits associated with subjective well-being could not have evolved if humans in the past were never happy, as the dark vision of *Better Angels* would have us believe.

Pinker has confused history with biography. In a rhetorical gesture of great power, he has invited the reader to imagine living a life that spanned the centuries from the Middle Ages to the present, like an immigrant leaving the horrors of the Third World for the comforts of America. But this is a phantom argument. Whole populations, across their generations, cannot have this experience. In every era, people calibrate their sense of well-being to the conditions of the day. Think of it this way: a hundred years hence, medicine may have cured our sneezes and our itches. But unless your great-grandchildren are lucky enough to experience this change during their lifetimes, it will not make them happier than you are. Although history can and does tell a story of constant structural change, in other words, subjective well-being is historically invariant. This important point has been made by Darrin McMahon, the historian of happiness.[26] The point is worth arguing, but if McMahon is right and Pinker is wrong, then long-term shifts in levels of violence can have no impact on aggregate levels of subjective well-being. The past was never a vale of tears, and no decline in violence will bring greater happiness.

By way of conclusion, the deep history of violence, if done right, will not privilege the aggressor at the expense of the victim. From the victims' point of view, violence is an inescapable feature of human life, even if, like sex or eating, the forms that it takes are variable. Deeply entangled in relations of power and dominance, violence is durable and protean. It operates in plain sight and also in the nooks and crannies of human relations. In light of the deep history of violence, it is incumbent upon us to be aware of the presence of violence, to recognize its forms, and to find ways to work against it.

Acknowledgments

I am grateful to Daniel Mroczek and Matthew Liebmann for their thoughts and suggestions and to the students of Anthropology/History 2059 for their insightful contributions to the broader themes of this essay.

Daniel Lord Smail is the Frank B. Baird, Jr. Professor of History at Harvard University. His current research approaches transformations in the material culture of later medieval Mediterranean Europe (1100–1600) using household inventories and inventories of debt collection from Lucca and Marseille. Recent books include Legal Plunder: Households and Debt Collection in Late Medieval Europe *(2016) and, with Andrew Shryock and others,* Deep History: The Architecture of Past and Present *(2011).*

Notes

1. Steven Pinker, *The Better Angels of Our Nature: Why Violence Has Declined* (New York: Viking, 2011); Steven Pinker, *Enlightenment Now: The Case for Reason, Science, Humanism, and Progress* (New York: Viking, 2018).
2. Other works include David Christian, *Maps of Time: An Introduction to Big History* (Berkeley: University of California Press, 2004); Felipe Fernández-Armesto, *Humankind: A Brief History* (Oxford: Oxford University Press, 2004); Yuval N. Harari, *Sapiens: A Brief History of Humankind* (London: Harvill Secker, 2014).
3. E.g., Nam C. Kim, "Angels, Illusions, Hydras, and Chimeras: Violence and Humanity," *Reviews in Anthropology* 41, no. 4 (2012): 239–272; R. Brian Ferguson, "Pinker's List: Exaggerating Prehistoric War Mortality," in *War, Peace, and Human Nature: The Convergence of Evolutionary and Cultural Views*, ed. Douglas P. Fry (Oxford: Oxford University Press, 2013), 112–131.
4. See also Robert M. Sapolsky, *Behave: The Biology of Humans at Our Best and Worst* (New York: Penguin, 2017).
5. Pinker, *Better Angels*, 361.
6. See the critical overview in David J. Buller, *Adapting Minds: Evolutionary Psychology and the Persistent Quest for Human Nature* (Cambridge, MA: MIT Press, 2005).
7. Steven Pinker, *How the Mind Works* (New York: Norton, 1997).
8. Jonathan Haidt, *The Righteous Mind: Why Good People Are Divided by Politics and Religion* (New York: Pantheon Books, 2012).
9. Barbara H. Rosenwein, "Problems and Methods in the History of Emotions," *Passions in Context: International Journal for the History and Theory of Emotions* 1 (2010), online, http://www.passionsincontext.de (accessed 16 March 2018).
10. Jan Plamper, *The History of Emotions: An Introduction*, trans. Keith Tribe (Oxford: Oxford University Press, 2015), 32–33.
11. Pinker, *Better Angels*, 132.
12. Ibid., 751.
13. Robert Held, Marcello Bertoni, and Amor Gil, *Inquisition: A Bilingual Guide to the Exhibition of Torture Instruments from the Middle Ages to the Industrial Era, Presented in Various European Cities in 1983–87* (Florence: Qua d'Arno, 1985), 14.
14. Among medieval historians, it is widely known that the supposed instruments of torture (a) postdate the Middle Ages and (b) are often fake. For a debunking of the "pear of anguish" (Pinker, *Better Angels*, p. 131; Held et al., *Inquisition*, pp. 132–133), see Chris Bishop, "The 'Pear of Anguish': Truth, Torture and Dark Medievalism," *International Journal of Cultural Studies* 17, no. 6 (2014): 591–602.
15. Daniel P. Mannix, *The History of Torture* (Phoenix Mill, UK: Sutton, 2003). For an obituary identifying his days as a carnival performer, see http://www.nytimes.com/1997/02/08/arts/daniel-mannix-85-adventure-writer.html (accessed 3 December 2017).
16. Sanford Levinson, "Contemplating Torture: An Introduction," in *Torture: A Collection*, ed. Sanford Levinson (Oxford: Oxford University Press, 2004), 23–43.
17. John H. Langbein, *Torture and the Law of Proof: Europe and England in the Ancien Régime* (Chicago: University of Chicago Press, 1977); Edward Peters, *Torture*, expanded ed. (Philadelphia: University of Pennsylvania Press, 1996).
18. Stephen Jay Gould, "Nonmoral Nature," *Natural History* 91, no. 2 (February 1982): 19–26, here 26.
19. See, e.g., Pinker, *Better Angels*, 497–509.

20. Peter Singer, *Animal Liberation: A New Ethics for Our Treatment of Animals* (New York: HarperCollins, 1975).

21. Bernard E. Harcourt, *Illusion of Order: The False Promise of Broken Windows Policing* (Cambridge, MA: Harvard University Press, 2001); Elizabeth Kai Hinton, *From the War on Poverty to the War on Crime: The Making of Mass Incarceration in America* (Cambridge, MA: Harvard University Press, 2016); Johan Galtung, "Violence, Peace, and Peace Research," *Journal of Peace Research* 6, no. 3 (1969): 167–191; Rob Nixon, *Slow Violence and the Environmentalism of the Poor* (Cambridge, MA: Harvard University Press, 2011).

22. See, inter alia, Jörg Niewöhner, "Epigenetics: Embedded Bodies and the Molecularisation of Biography and Milieu," *BioSocieties* 6, no. 3 (13 June 2011): 279–298.

23. Amartya Sen, *Development as Freedom* (New York: Knopf, 1999), 21–24.

24. David G. Myers and Ed Diener, "Who Is Happy?," *Psychological Science* 6, no. 1 (1995): 10–19; David Lykken and Auke Tellegen, "Happiness Is a Stochastic Phenomenon," *Psychological Science* 7, no. 3 (1996): 186–189; Robert A. Cummins, "Can Happiness Change? Theories and Evidence," in *Stability of Happiness: Theories and Evidence on Whether Happiness Can Change,* ed. Kennon M. Sheldon and Richard E. Lucas (London: Academic Press, 2014), 75–97. For criticisms of set point theory, see Bruce Headey, "The Set-Point Theory of Well-Being Needs Replacing: On the Brink of a Scientific Revolution?," *SSRN Electronic Journal,* 2007, doi:10.2139/ssrn.1096451; Richard E. Lucas, "Adaptation and the Set-Point Model of Subjective Well-Being," *Current Directions in Psychological Science* 16, no. 2 (2007): 75–79.

25. Philip Brickman, Dan Coates, and Ronnie Janoff-Bulman, "Lottery Winners and Accident Victims: Is Happiness Relative?," *Journal of Personality and Social Psychology* 36, no. 8 (1978): 917–927.

26. Darrin M. McMahon, *Happiness: A History* (New York: Atlantic Monthly Press, 2006), 466–480.

Chapter 11

What Pinker Leaves Out

Mark S. Micale

When, in 2011, I first reviewed *The Better Angels of Our Nature: The Decline of Violence in History and Its Causes*,[1] I was struck by author Steven Pinker's sins of commission. Throughout this very long book, the author cherry-picked examples to advance his thesis; alternately idealized and stigmatized entire past eras; and continually dismissed masses of counter-evidence. Every page seemed to sport an overgeneralization as Pinker rode roughshod over the complexities and qualifications that a convincing account of the history of human violence would seem to require. Instead of localized, contextualized knowledge about the human past and an acknowledgment of the specificities of place and time—the bread and butter of professional historians—*Better Angels* advanced a severely reductive thesis that could not possibly be squared with the atrocities of the twentieth century and implied a naïve, perhaps irresponsible, understanding of the present. Pinker's use of historiography was skimpy and tendentious throughout.[2]

Returning to the book several years later, I am more struck by what it leaves out. Pinker's omissions, I now see, are not simply details that might have added narrative texture or case studies that might have fleshed out his interpretations empirically. They are, rather, significant conceptual absences, deficiencies in Pinker's basic view of the central subject. Cumulatively, these silences make for a flawed and limited thesis that is a vast oversimplification, if not a fundamental misinterpretation.

First of all, Pinker's work exhibits an overly Western outlook. "The West and the rest" is a mentality much on display in his pages. Pinker draws the great majority of his historical data from Europe—particularly Central and Western Europe, including Great Britain—and North America. Virtually all the agencies of nonviolence he identifies (printing, the Enlightenment, religious humanitarianism, progressive legal codes, etc.) began in a dozen or so Western countries. The table of contents actually includes subchapters on "the rest of the world" in the wake of discussions of developments in Britain, France, and the United States. His history of violence is set entirely in the northern hemisphere, implying that the progressive trends originating there are radiating outward to the rest of the planet—or will eventually do so.

In this light, it is not surprising that Pinker largely neglects human violence associated with imperialism. In his extensive quantitative analysis of the history of modern military conflicts, wars that were fought in Africa, South America, and Asia (except regarding Japan in World War II) figure very little. He relies heavily on the idea of "the long peace," which supposedly reigned from Napoleon's defeat in 1815 to World War I; he is apparently unfamiliar with the important colonialist critique that has been made against this thesis. Even if we limit the study of imperialism to conflicts involving Britain, hundreds of thousands of colonial subjects were killed in Australia, Afghanistan, China, the Falklands, India, Jamaica, Kenya, New Zealand, and South Africa, in what Byron Farwell has termed "Queen Victoria's little wars."[3] The six-month Anglo-Zulu War of 1879, which led to Britain's destruction of the Zulu Kingdom, never gets a mention from Pinker.[4] Caroline Elkins, in her powerful essay, copiously documents widespread, systematic use of "legalized lawlessness" in British colonies from Palestine to Kenya after World War II. To use only one event in South American history as an example, Pinker does not cite, much less consider, the Paraguayan War of the 1860s, a devastating six-year conflict that did away with nearly 70 percent of Paraguay's adult males.

Because such losses did not occur in the westernmost section of the Eurasian landmass, they seem to count for little in Pinker's thinking. Even regarding Russia and China, the Taiping Rebellion in southern China (1850–1864) and the Russian Civil War that followed the Bolshevik Revolution receive only passing mentions. But many military historians regard the Russian Civil War to be the bloodiest civil war of the twentieth century. The 14-year Taiping Rebellion resulted, by conservative estimates, in 20–30 million deaths. Pinker mentions the massacres following the partitioning of India and Pakistan in 1947 in only a single parenthetical comment, giving no indication of the level of carnage associated with these Hindu-Muslim riots.[5]

And what of the scores of anticolonial struggles that punctuated the twentieth century? Anti-Spanish and anti-Portuguese wars of independence in Latin American during the first half of the 1800s and anticolonial insurgencies in Africa during the 1950s and 1960s appear in a few of the myriad charts and lists assembled by Pinker. These events, however, seem wholly peripheral to his overall interpretation that centers on "great power" confrontations within Europe. Pinker seems unaware of an interpretative sea change that has been growing the past generation among historians: the emerging view that, like the two world wars and the Nazi Holocaust, decolonialization ranks among the most important historical processes of the twentieth century. The Algerian War for Independence (1954–1962), notorious for torture practiced by both the French and the Algerian FLN and the prototype of violent anticolonial warfare, receives only single-sentence citations.[6] In *Better Angels*, there is no indication that Pinker is aware of the burgeoning imperial, colonial, and postcolonial historiographies considered by many practitioners to be the most significant scholarly development of the past generation.

Linked to Pinker's systematic undervaluation of imperial/colonial violence is his underappraisal of indigeneity, the second major silence in the book. The cultural modernity that Pinker champions as the source of diminishing violence in our time has very much been a game of historical winners and losers. We know that at least since the dying out of the Neanderthals in Ice Age Europe, roughly between 40,000 and 24,000 years ago, waves of migrating, anatomically modern *Homo sapiens* from Africa have played a role, whether direct or indirect, in driving other hominid populations into extinction. How many unrecorded genocides from the prehistoric past are lost to human memory we will probably never know. By the same token, one need only mention certain countries—Indonesia, Cambodia, and Rwanda, above all—to be reminded of genocidal violence during the past half century in which both the victims and perpetrators were non-Western. Nonetheless, there is no doubt that the extermination or near extermination of indigenous peoples accelerated hugely when, beginning at the close of the fifteenth century, Europeans arrived in the Americas, Asia, and Australia.

The past generation has witnessed an outpouring of historical scholarship on this phenomenon. Charles C. Mann's sobering pair of recent books, *1491* and *1493*, documents in heartbreaking detail the fate of millions of pre-Columbian Indians in Mexico and Central America and the demise of their astonishing civilizations during a single generation following 1492.[7] Theft of native lands, conflicts with European town dwellers, cultural domination, economic exploitation, forced migration, enslavement, lethal new diseases, and finally extinction or near extinction: with local variations, these tragic processes would be repeated across the globe upon European contact, expansion, and settlement. The story of the decimation of Australian, especially Tasmanian, Aborigines, mostly at the hands of early British colonists, is too well-known to need repeating. Concerning US history, Benjamin Madley's *An American Genocide* is the most recent, authoritative reconstruction of the story of the eradication of the Northern California Indians during the "Mendocino Wars" in the decade following the discovery of gold in 1848.[8]

Figuring out whether a violent event in the past deserves "the G-word" is often controversial.[9] Whatever terms we choose to describe the facts, it is clear that the destruction of entire communities of indigenous peoples by foreign conquerors, usually for a combination of economic and religious motives, was carried out during Europe's "long peace" by some of the same Western countries that Pinker salutes for spreading peace-beneficial practices. Just as problematically, and paradoxically, large-scale and systematic destruction of non-European peoples and cultures during the past five centuries was often done in the name of "civilizing the natives" or a *mission civilatrice,* introducing Christianity, capitalism, and Western culture to supposedly pagan and primitive peoples. Although Pinker cites some anthropological literature on indigenous populations in his bibliography, the book indicates little awareness of the growing literature produced by our profession on this subject.

The third category missing from Pinker's provocative argument that the current era is the most peaceful time in history is violence against animals. Some readers may think it too outré to include human-animal violence in the analysis, yet Pinker himself devotes considerable attention to the treatment of animals on the basis that one of the founding beliefs of humane societies is that animal violence is closely linked to human violence. In a chapter called "The Rights Revolution," Pinker includes a 20-page excursus on "animal rights and the decline of cruelty to animals."[10] He notes the rise of the animal rights movement in America, the campaign for no-kill dog kennels, the outlawing of bull fights in some regions of Spain, the criminalization of cockfighting, the removal of elephants, lions, and tigers from traveling circuses, and other advances. He also states that hunting as a pastime is on the decline.

These are historically significant developments indeed. In fact, my sense is that Pinker actually underestimates how great a transformation in sensibility is represented by the growing strength of animal-human bonds and the enrichment of cross-species relationships. But, before my fellow animal lovers and I uncork our champagne bottles in celebration, let us again consider what Pinker excludes from his thesis. Chief among the omissions, there is no discussion whatsoever of two particular groups: wildlife and agricultural animals.

In arguing that animals are treated better today than ever before, Pinker mainly has in mind house pets (primarily cats and dogs) and horses. These, of course, are domesticated animals bred by people for sport, recreation, and companionship. Even regarding dogs, zoologists, pet food researchers, and various government agencies estimate that between 75 and 80 percent of the world canine population consists of free-ranging animals, both in rural and urban settings, rather than pets.[11] Largely ignored are farm animals and wild animals, which of course massively outnumber indoor companion pets. According to the World Population Clock, the planet's human population as of 20 January 2018 stood at 7.45 billion; the largest majority of these humans are carnivores.

Pinker adores statistics, so here is a set of them he could profitably contemplate: in a single month, December 2017, as reported by the United States Department of Agriculture (USDA), the number of animals slaughtered for food included 2.58 million beef cattle, 46,400 calves (for veal), 10.5 million hogs, and 188,100 lambs. In 2008, the last year the USDA published annual "slaughter totals," the number included 35.5 million cattle, 116.5 million pigs, 271.2 million turkeys, and 2.4 million rabbits. By far the largest slaughter each year involves chickens, with a staggering 9,075,261,000 in 2008. These are the figures of animals killed just to feed meat-eating Americans in one year.[12]

Reliable global statistics on the slaughter of farm animals are difficult to obtain; many countries do not keep or share records. In 2004, however, the Food and Agriculture Organization (FAO) put together estimates derived from reports published in more than 210 countries and territories around the world. The FAO estimated that in 2003 the slaughter included: 4 million horses, 292 million cows and calves, 345 million goats, 691 million turkeys, 857 million rabbits, 2.3 billion ducks, and 45.9 billion chickens.[13] Most of this killing involves assembly-line, factory-style killing in "animal processing centers." Vastly more animals per year are now killed for human consumption than at any previous time in human history.[14]

Pinker accuses the news media of grossly amplifying the extent of violence today, but the industrial-scale killing of animals for food is a form of violence that the media rarely covers—or even regards as an issue. Nevertheless, in any up-to-date account of violence in the world, the fate of billions of sentient farm animals requires serious moral reckoning. The history of animals also happens to be one of the newest areas of historical scholarship today. Young scholars tend to be especially interested in the idea of historicizing human-animal relations. Pinker shows no signs of being aware of this development.

And what of undomesticated animals living in nature? The intricately detailed 30-page index to *The Better Angels of Our Nature* contains no entry for "wildlife." I doubt this is editorial oversight. The fate of animals living in nature simply cannot be reconciled with Pinker's thesis. It is crystal clear that capitalist consumerism and the explosive growth of human population, when combined with ever more powerful technologies, have been singularly disastrous for untold numbers of animal species. As the prehistoric fate of certain big mammals—such as the Siberian woolly mammoth, the American mastodon, and Australia's ancient megafauna—attests, early humans were capable of driving entire species into oblivion long before the Industrial Revolution. The rate of animal extinctions has been tremendously accelerated, however, with the coming of the age of machines—that is, with the advent of technological modernity.

At present, the two greatest threats to wildlife are rapid climate change and ecosystem decimation, both of which are caused largely or entirely by humans. In the first instance, animals are endangered by human-induced damage to natural environments, especially by the burning of fossil fuels into the atmosphere. In other instances, wild animals are victimized directly by hunters killing for sport, by poachers killing for money, by farmers killing animals with traps and guns, and by developers destroying microhabitats that wildlife depend upon, to name only a few of the sources.

It is a disturbing irony that Pinker draws his theoretical underpinnings for understanding human nature from Darwinian psychology. In recent years, "extinction studies" have emerged as a new international domain of inquiry in the disciplines of evolutionary and ecological biology as well as among humanities scholars. The message is dire. Damage to the planetary biomass is not limited to the most beautiful and majestic species and places, such as elephants, polar bears, and the Great Barrier Reef. The threat is far more widespread, with potentially grave consequences.

In the English-speaking world, Elizabeth Kolbert's Pulitzer Prize–winning volume *The Sixth Extinction* is perhaps the most sobering and high-profile statement of the crisis. Kolbert shows unmistakably that the diversity of life-forms on our planet is diminishing dramatically. The drastic loss extends across the plant and animal kingdoms, to marine and terrestrial ecosystems; it is occurring on every continent, impinging on hundreds of thousands of species.[15] Many life scientists consider the massive die-off to be the most urgent issue of our time. To some readers, this phenomenon may seem rather far removed from the topic of Pinker's book, but to others it will be pressingly relevant. For if, as Kolbert writes, "our historical moment is one of the unprecedented loss of planetary life forms," and if, as a consensus among scientists tells us, this multifaceted process is caused by human-propelled environmental degradation, in what sense are we living in the most peaceful of historical times?

In returning now to a more traditional form of human violence—warfare and military technology—and its relation to Pinker's thesis, I especially want to consider, at somewhat greater length, weapons of mass destruction. In his lengthy chapter on "the long peace," Pinker includes a section on "nuclear peace theory."[16] The title and placement of this discussion indicate how he views the subject. For Pinker, as for many defense policy makers and American citizens today, nuclear arsenals have played a key role in preventing the half-century-long "Cold War" from ever becoming "hot"; they were also one reason why the United States prevailed in the epic confrontation between the democratic West and the communist East. Because a full-scale attack and counterattack with nuclear bombs between the superpowers would have obliterated the populations of both superpowers, and might have further risked the survival of the human species through an environmental "nuclear winter," these weapons have been credited with deterring all-out military confrontations between the United States, the USSR, and China—although they did not prevent bloody proxy wars.

What most strikes Pinker about the destruction of Hiroshima and Nagasaki in August 1945 is that the atomic bombs were exploded to end a war and have not been deployed since. In his presentation, the Cuban missile crisis of 1962 was, above all, a learning experience in which cooler heads prevailed; it taught the United States and the Soviet Union to avoid further brinksmanship. Pinker acknowledges that, by the 1980s, the nuclear "arms race" had peaked, obscenely, with some 70,000 weapons in global arsenals, many of them targeted at enemy nations and set on computerized trigger alert, but he is impressed by the nuclear freeze movement that this tense situation sparked and by the arms reduction talks that took place and the nonproliferation treaties that were signed. He also reminds us that, at the dawn of the nuclear age in the mid-1940s, the Manhattan Project helped the free world defeat both German fascism and Japanese imperialism.

Unavoidably, our retrospective analysis of the Cold War reflects our personal politics. Nevertheless, whatever our understanding of that period in international affairs, its conclusion in 1990 assuredly did not bring the end of the nuclear story. With the sudden and unexpected collapse of the Soviet Union, and then the relatively nonviolent end of the Soviet presence in East Germany and Eastern Europe, the "nuclear peril" all but disappeared from public consciousness. This public response is perhaps understandable: after all, since the 1990s no enemy power of the magnitude of Nazi Germany, imperial Japan, or Stalin's Soviet Union has had the capacity to threaten Western liberal democracies. Such reassuring assumptions, however, are misguided, because our current postcommunist world is far from nuclear-free. The Cold War's end ushered in "a second nuclear age," an era in some ways both similar to and different from the first phase of nuclear history.[17] This second nuclear age, in which we all now live, Pinker fails to ponder, although the late Jonathan Schell, whose great lifelong project was raising global human consciousness about the realities of a nuclear-armed world, explored it in penetrating detail for decades.[18]

The Cold War's sudden end offered a historic opportunity to ban nuclear weapons worldwide. A successful international effort to do so, Schell observed, would have been a momentous achievement. But old mental and military habits die hard, and the political will required for such a comprehensive elimination did not materialize. In the years after the Cold War, a New Agenda Coalition consisting of seven governments (Brazil, Egypt, Ireland, Mexico, New Zealand, Sweden, and South Africa) bravely called for dismantling nuclear weaponry everywhere. Between 1989 and 1991, South Africa voluntarily destroyed its own fledgling nuclear weapons program; it remains the only nation to have completely denuclearized of its own accord. The seven "oldest" nuclear countries—the United States, the Russian Federation, Britain, France, China, India, and Israel—however, did not do so.

As Schell has highlighted, the US government's original motives for acquiring nuclear arms—beating Nazi physicists to the bomb, ending the Pacific war faster, and containing communism—became obsolete. In fact, as early as 1945 some Manhattan Project scientists, as well as Albert Einstein, argued for terminating the production program when Germany surrendered on 7 May of that year. Instead, the several nations that formed the original "nuclear club" all decided to retain their arsenals. In the United States, this became policy under both Republican and Democratic presidents. As Schell saw, in the second nuclear age, atomic weapons have become an established, permanent feature of the security apparatus of several nations.

So, a quarter century after the end of the Cold War, what does the worldwide nuclear situation look like? In strict statistical terms, arms reductions since the 1990s have been dramatic. Still, the latest report from the Stockholm International Peace Research Institute says that there are currently between 14,900 and 15,000 nuclear weapons across the planet. These warheads can be delivered from air, land, and sea. The United States and Russia, which possess by far the largest arsenals, maintain roughly 6,800 nuclear weapons apiece on high-alert status, ready to be launched within minutes. Most of these are many times more powerful than the friendly sounding "Little Boy" and "Fat Man" bombs that fell on Japan. Moreover, China, India, and Pakistan are believed to be adding to their stockpiles. Most nuclear nations continually modernize their warheads and enhance the computerized systems that target, launch, and guide them. Five other European nations, including Turkey, host NATO weapons on their soil that are controlled by one of the nuclear powers. Twenty-three additional countries, many in Eastern Europe, are "nuclear umbrella" nations, meaning that at least one nuclear arms–possessing nation is required by treaty to defend them if they are attacked.

Given their awesome destructive power, the number of nuclear weapons deployed around the world remains formidable; in truth, what has reduced is only the degree of "nuclear redundancy"—or, in Schellian terms, the degree to which we could destroy all human life on the planet many times over. As a consequence, we need to soberly ask ourselves: how does the current nuclear situation stack up against what existed during the Cold War? Without a single, massively armed state opponent, a "third world war"—detonation of hundreds or thousands of weapons from both sides capable of annihilating most of humanity—seems to be much less likely than it was from 1945 through 1990. Beyond this base standard, the conditions of Schell's "second nuclear age" are not comforting.

Since 1990, the family of nuclear powers has enlarged. Unsurprisingly, the decision of the most established nuclear nations to maintain their arsenals has encouraged other nations to acquire nuclear weapons as they strive to make their way in a tense, competitive world. Pakistan obtained nuclear capability in 1998, and North Korea did so in the past few years, bringing the number of nations so equipped to nine. Iran developed an extensive nuclear infrastructure that is now being monitored closely. Since nuclear weapons were first engineered in the Arizona desert in 1945, they have proliferated to other countries at a rate of about one nation every eight years. As historians of science have repeatedly demonstrated, it is in the nature of new technology to spread and eventually become universal.

Especially striking is the geography of the new nuclear powers in the postcommunist world. Pakistan and North Korea, as well as Israel, Iran, and Turkey, are located in some of the world's most volatile spots: the Arab Middle East, South Asia, and the Korean Peninsula. The USSR and the United States were on separate continents half a world apart. Despite their historic rivalry, the two managed for decades to negotiate their differences without resorting to a nuclear attack. They conducted local wars—the United States in Vietnam, the Soviet Union in Afghanistan, and China in various border wars—with restraint on the nuclear front.

In contrast, India and Pakistan, the two Koreas, and Israel and its Arab neighbors are all much smaller nations (except for India) situated close to their enemies. In some places, these states share contested territorial borders with their antagonists, a situation akin to Europe's powers in the era of the two world wars. Perhaps most worrisome, their animosities take the form of ancient blood feuds often involving religious passions. Since winning independence in 1947, India and Pakistan have made war with each other four times. In 1998 and 2001, Indo-Pakistani nuclear confrontations had to be defused by emergency visits from American secretaries of state. The newest nuclear state, North Korea, is widely deemed to be the world's worst totalitarian dictatorship. As this chapter is being written, at least three nuclear nations—North Korea, Turkey, and the United States—are headed by political leaders with erratic personalities prone to bellicose rhetoric.[19]

In his final book, *The Seventh Decade: The New Shape of Nuclear Danger,* in 2007, Schell attempted to integrate into his thinking the 9/11 attacks on New York and Washington, DC, as well as the Bush/Cheney/Rumsfeld "global war on Islamic terrorism" and retaliatory attacks in cities such as Mumbai, Madrid, and London.[20] This latest form of barbarism, he pointed out, has been stateless and therefore has fewer resources at its command. On the other hand, it has few reservations. Crucially, the new global terrorism lacks the rational means-to-ends restraints of national governments; it seeks misanthropically to kill as many people in as spectacular a way as possible. Its interest in obtaining the ultimate weapon, and its willingness to use it, propel the nuclear threat into new territory.

This focus on the nuclear arsenals of the globe, I would add, excludes from consideration chemical and biological weapons, the first of which were banned by international law after World War I but have been deployed since the 1980s in Japan, Iraq, Syria, and elsewhere. Neither have I raised the newest issue: the criminal hacking of government computer systems by either domestic or foreign actors.

A number of contributors to this book have criticized Pinker's book for its cramped, overly quantitative criteria of historical violence, focusing narrowly on such things as official statistics on deaths from wars between states and on domestic murders. In its place, they have proposed alternative criteria, at once more interesting and sophisticated, for studying the subject, including Daniel Smail's novel idea of looking at the victim's subjective experiences of violence and how these change over time.

Here is a small thought experiment: let us imagine that just once in the next 25 years, somewhere on Earth, a single nuclear weapon of average megatonnage is fired. The possibility of such an event is not far-fetched in light of the geopolitical conditions and circumstances that prevail in the world. Assuming the explosion is not accidental—that it is not caused by human or mechanical error—the weapon will likely be aimed to inflict maximum damage. It would surely kill at least a million, and possibly several million, and there would be continuing loss of life for years to come. In "A Republic of Insects and Grasses," the first chapter of *The Fate of the Earth,* Schell reconstructed unforgettably the sheer physical horror of such a weapon exploding over Lower Manhattan.

If such an event occurred, what effect would it have on Pinker's thinking? Would Pinker argue the event away as such a statistical rarity that it proved the rule? Or would he perhaps calculate that, in proportion to the planet's total population, the carnage would still be historically negligible?

Instead of accepting Pinker's criteria, let me propose that the ultimate measure of a society's level of violence is its *killing capability.* By this yardstick, nuclear weapons are far and away the most lethal instrument of violence ever created. The governments of any of the nine nations now maintaining operational nuclear weapons have the capacity to inflict mass mortality on a scale and with a speed that would have been unimaginable to Caligula, Genghis Khan, or Napoleon.

And here we encounter another irony: the premodern periods in the human past that Pinker caricatures as ranking among the most primitively pugilistic—those of the prehistoric period, the ancient Mediterranean, and Europe's medieval centuries—had nothing even remotely approaching today's capacity for technological mayhem. On the contrary, those earlier societies emerge as among the least violent! Rocks, clubs, and stone hatchets; swords, spears, and catapults; lances, crossbows, and ball and chain weapons—these are like cap guns compared to a nuclear missile.

If we prefer, we can use an event from the American national memory as the basis of comparison. One of the bloodiest battles fought on American soil was the Battle of Gettysburg, which raged between 1 July and 3 July 1863. The combined death toll on the Union and Confederate sides was approximately 7,500. The victims were male combatants who were felled by rifle shot, cannon fire, and hand-to-hand combat. After the hostilities ceased, the bodies of the dead were identified and buried, either at a local cemetery (which Lincoln consecrated inspiringly) or transported home for burial by their families.[21] Only one civilian is known to have been killed.[22]

Now contrast the toll at Gettysburg to the catastrophe of a single nuclear blast. In an attack on a city, millions would perish; the largest number would be vaporized within the first 20 seconds after ignition. Others would become corpses, instantaneously charred beyond recognition. Most of the casualties would be civilians, including children. Another additional untold number would suffer the horrid short-term or long-term effects of acute radiation poisoning. Most likely, the dead would have been killed by a single technician, far from the site of the explosion, presumably someone who pushed a button, obeying the instructions of a political leader. Is ours, then, the most peaceful of times or the most violent of times?

To compare with any meaning and accuracy a phenomenon as complex as human aggression over seven thousand years of human history and across all world cultures is an impossible task. As several contributors demonstrate, we lack anything like a stable and coherent source base that would enable us to make reliable statistical measurements of this subject on a long-term, cross-cultural basis. The categories and the very meaning of violence have changed profoundly over time and no doubt will continue changing in the future.

To reiterate, no in-depth history of violence can ignore violence in the categories I define as colonial, indigenous, biological, environmental, and technological. If a history of violence were written from the perspective of a subjugated former colony, rather than from the vantage point of a conquering nation, how would it read? What good is the gradual decline of violence among certain classes of human beings in some regions of the globe if your own people, culture, and language have ceased to exist? Is it possible to reconcile the Pinker Thesis with the crisis of specicide unfolding today in the animal kingdom? Why are we celebrating peacefulness in our time when 15,000 weapons of mass destruction remain ready to be launched in our highly conflict-ridden world? Answers to these questions—indeed, the questions themselves—are fatally absent from Steven Pinker's big, attention-grabbing tome.

Mark S. Micale is Emeritus Professor of History at the University of Illinois in Urbana-Champaign. His fields of specialization are modern European intellectual history, post-Revolutionary France, the history of medicine and science, and masculinity studies. He is the author or editor of seven books, including Beyond the Unconscious, Discovering the History of Psychiatry, Traumatic Pasts: History, Psychiatry, and Trauma in the Modern Age, 1870–1930, The Mind of Modernism, *and* Hysterical Men: The Hidden History of Male Nervous Illness.

Notes

1. Steven Pinker, *The Better Angels of Our Nature: The Decline of Violence in History and Its Causes* (London: Allen Lane, 2011).
2. Mark S. Micale, "Improvements," review of Steven Pinker, *The Better Angels of Our Nature: The Decline of Violence in History and Its Causes, Times Literary Supplement*, no. 5684 (9 March 2012).
3. Byron Farwell, *Queen Victoria's Little Wars* (New York: Norton, 1985); Ian Hernon, *Massacre and Retribution: Forgotten Wars of the 19th Century* (Stroud: Sutton, 1998); Ian Hernon, *The Savage Empire: Forgotten Wars of the 19th Century* (Stroud: Sutton Publishing, 2000); Peter Turchin, *War and Peace and War: The Life Cycles of Imperial Nations* (New York: Pi, 2005).
4. James O. Gump, *The Dust Rose Like Smoke: The Subjugation of the Zulu and the Sioux*, 2nd ed. (Lincoln: University of Nebraska Press, 2016).
5. Pinker, *Better Angels*, 383.

6. Marnia Lazreg, *Torture and the Twilight of Empire: From Algiers to Baghdad* (Princeton, NJ: Princeton University Press, 2008).

7. Charles C. Mann, *1491: New Revelations of the Americas before Columbus* (New York: Vintage Books, 2006); Charles C. Mann, *1493: Uncovering the New World Columbus Created* (New York: Knopf, 2011).

8. Benjamin Madley, *An American Genocide: The United States and the California Indian Catastrophe, 1846–1873* (New Haven, CT: Yale University Press, 2016).

9. For a measured critique of this term in Australian history, see Philip Dwyer and Lyndall Ryan, "Reflections on Genocide and Settler-Colonial Violence," *History Australia* 13, no. 2 (2016): 335–350.

10. Pinker, *Better Angels*, 454–475.

11. Regarding dogs, see Hilda Kean, *The Great Cat and Dog Massacre: The Real Story of World War Two's Unknown Tragedy* (Chicago: University of Chicago Press, 2017) for the shocking story of 400,000 pet dogs and cats in the London region that were euthanized over four days in September 1939 following the outbreak of war between Britain and Germany.

12. Statistics cited from https://www.nass.usda.gov/Surveys/Guide_to_NASS_Sur veys/Livestock_Slaughter/ and http://www.humanesociety.org/news/resources/ research/stats_slaughter_totals.html?referrer=https://search.yahoo.com/ (accessed 7 January 2018).

13. https://www.upc-online.org/slaughter/92704stats.htm (accessed 8 January 2018).

14. I leave to another time the related issue of industrial fishing in the open oceans, including seafloor trawling, which collects thousands of tons of fish annually, as well as large-scale commercial aquaculture.

15. Elizabeth Kolbert, *Sixth Extinction: An Unnatural History* (London: Bloomsbury, 2014).

16. Pinker, *Better Angels*, 268–278.

17. Jonathan Schell, *The Seventh Decade: The New Shape of Nuclear Danger* (New York: Henry Holt and Company, 2007), 201–223.

18. Jonathan Schell, *The Fate of the Earth* (New York: Alfred A. Knopf, 1982); Jonathan Schell, *The Jonathan Schell Reader* (New York: Nation Books, 2004), Part II, "The Nuclear Dilemma," 57–211; Jonathan Schell, *The Unconquerable World: Power, Nonviolence, and the Will of the People* (London: Allen Lane, 2003); Jonathan Schell, "The Unfinished Twentieth-Century: What We Have Forgotten about Nuclear Weapons," *Harper's Magazine*, January 2000, 41–55; Jonathan Schell, *The Unfinished Twentieth Century: The Crisis of Weapons of Mass Destruction* (London: Verso, 2001); Schell, *The Seventh Decade* (2007).

19. In his State of the Union address delivered on 4 February 2018, President Donald Trump called on Congress to "modernize and rebuild our nuclear arsenal" in response to Russia's alleged nuclear buildup under President Vladimir Putin. Estimated cost of such a modernization: $1.2 trillion. See David E. Sanger and William J. Broad, "U.S. Chases Russia into New Arms Race as a Treaty Takes Effect," *New York Times*, 5 February 2018.

20. Schell, *Seventh Decade*.

21. John W. Busey and David G. Martin, *Regimental Strengths and Losses at Gettysburg*, 4th ed. (Highstown, NJ: Longstreet House, 2005), http://www.historynet.com/ gettysburg-casualties (accessed 26 December 2017).

22. Patsy Halbur, "Jennie Wade and Gettysburg: It Was Not Supposed to Happen," *Gettysburg Magazine* 25 (July 2001): 105–115.

Index

CPSIA information can be obtained
at www.ICGtesting.com
Printed in the USA
JSHW010713140220
4234JS00006B/13